H Lafferty
2001

£1.50 ＊ ⑩
£3
52

KV-436-454

**Making
Change
pen**

For two very special people:
Bob Foster, brother and friend,
and
Sandi Borden, sister and soulmate.

Making Change Happen

Practical Planning for School Leaders

Jerry J. Herman
Janice L. Herman

CORWIN PRESS, INC.
A Sage Publications Company
Thousand Oaks, California

Copyright © 1994 by Corwin Press, Inc.

All rights reserved. No part of this book may be reproduced or utilized in any form or by any means, electronic or mechanical, including photocopying, recording, or by any information storage and retrieval system, without permission in writing from the publisher.

For information address:

Corwin Press, Inc.
A Sage Publications Company
2455 Teller Road
Thousand Oaks, California 91320

SAGE Publications Ltd.
6 Bonhill Street
London EC2A 4PU
United Kingdom

SAGE Publications India Pvt. Ltd.
M-32 Market
Greater Kailash I
New Delhi 110 048 India

Printed in the United States of America

Library of Congress Cataloging-in-Publication Data

Herman, Jerry John. 1930-
    Making change happen: practical planning for school leaders/
Jerry J. Herman, Janice L. Herman.
        p. cm.
    Includes bibliographical references and index.
    ISBN 0-8039-6096-4 (cl.) — ISBN 0-8039-6097-2 (pbk.)
    1. School management and organization—United States.
2. Educational planning—United States. 3. Educational change—
United States. I. Herman, Janice L.   II. Title.
LB2805.H417 1994   93-27064
371.2'00973—dc20

95 96 97 10 9 8 7 6 5 4 3 2

Corwin Press Production Editor: Rebecca Holland

Contents

Preface

Why Was This Book Written?

School districts and individual school buildings operate within an environment that is dynamic, open, and ever-changing. New laws are passed, financial support varies, pressure groups lobby for their desired change agendas, employee unions negotiate for changes, and boards of education demand changes.

Across this nation cries for changes in the ways schools are conducting their business are discussed daily in personal conversations, in the media, and in the chambers of federal and state legislatures. Some of the most visible terms currently being utilized to highlight the desired directions of change include:

- Restructuring
- Empowerment
- Choice
- Outcome-based
- Accountability
- Equity

Within this highly emotional and change-impacted educational environment exist the traditional positional leaders who carry the title of superintendent, principal, assistant superintendent, manager, and director. If these traditional leaders are reactive, or if they are insufficiently knowledgeable about change and tactical planning, they will, at best, be saddled with the management of changes demanded and initiated by others. If, however, these leaders are knowledgeable and proactive, they will ensure that all changes will move in positive directions toward effective schools.

Superintendents, principals, and other school leaders must become attuned to the pressures for change and must be prepared to provide the leadership that will direct these changes in a manner that will both strengthen their school districts and school buildings and bring about a high level of success. To effectively perform their leadership functions, these leaders must possess a thorough knowledge of a wide variety of planning techniques. To lead, they must also:

- recognize trends
- have a keen sense of timing
- possess a clear, guiding vision and a clear mission
- develop ownership by a majority of the schools' stakeholders
- direct resources in a manner designed to obtain the desired goals and outcomes
- clearly lead the direction of change
- most important, possess knowledge of and skill in planning for success

What Is This Book About?

This book is about administrators and other leaders creating change, using a wide variety of practical planning tools designed to assist educational leaders in their responsibility to develop and maintain successful schools. Such a tactical planning process, in serving the operationalizing of an overall strategic plan, is both long- and short-term. The strategic planning process, as a long-term concept and a guiding conceptual framework, is a consistent theme throughout the chapters. With that constant structure in place as a mindset and reference point, the yearly operational/tactical planning that executes the strategies and facilitates the desired outcomes of the strategic plan becomes the arena for day-to-day action. The accompanying specific planning strategies and tactics described in the text are intended to serve as a professional skill repertoire—a resource bank—for the planner/practitioner. The planning structures presented here have been infused with current restructuring concepts (effective schools research, school-based management, and Total Quality Management, or TQM) within the field of education to create a holistic model and framework for administrative thinking and planning. The text is therefore designed for use as a day-to-day reference guidebook for those educational leaders—superintendents, principals, and other administrators—who are responsible for and accountable to direct change in a manner that improves the operations and outputs of their school districts and their school buildings.

What Is the Structure of This Book?

Chapter 1 discusses why contemporary leadership is crucial to causing planned changes that will lead to successful schools. Given that assumption, Chapter 2 provides an overview of planning in schools to achieve a desired vision. It describes, in line-administrator language, the relationship between the whats and the hows of planning. The next planning step of mustering support for the planning effort is described in Chapter 3, which provides information related to the various roles schools' stakeholders play in the planning process, and it relates specific techniques for reaching consensus.

Gathering crucial planning input data and obtaining a state-of-the-district profile is outlined in Chapter 4, which discusses helpful overview techniques for administrators to use in their schools in developing basic planning information. More task-specific and situational strategies are described in Chapter 5, presenting a wide variety of specifically detailed tactical planning aids that are highly usable in educational settings.

Three chapters incorporate current restructuring strategies into the planning process in order to produce a cohesive and contemporary planning and change effort. Chapter 6 develops tactical administrative plans and implementation strategies related to the findings of effective schools' research. Chapter 7 develops tactical plans related to school-based management, the most popular restructuring program. Since planning is an essential prerequisite for successful implementation of school-based management, the vital steps are outlined in administrative terms. Chapter 8 develops tactical plans related to TQM. This promising change program is becoming a new watchword in school administration.

Chapter 9 presents the glue that ties strategy to tactic to management to evaluation—creating a total workable package for administrators. This book is liberally sprinkled with examples and checklists. A glossary and a list of references are also included.

For Whom Is This Book Written?

Leaders must lead by planning for improved quality, which in turn leads to successful schools. This book is written for those building principals, superintendents of schools, and those other categories of school leaders who are not satisfied to simply play the role of managers, but wish to become individuals who successfully lead their schools and school districts. These leaders intend to accomplish this by successful planning and by leading the school district's stakeholders who comprise the human elements of their individual school buildings and school districts.

Although this book is primarily written for building principals, superintendents of schools, and other educational leaders, it will also prove to be a helpful guidebook in graduate-level university courses in educational administration, for board of education members who hold the responsibility for establishing policies that will ensure successful schools, and for those individuals who are true students of planning and of education.

Jerry J. Herman, Ph.D.
Janice L. Herman, Ph.D.

About the Authors

Jerry J. Herman is a professor in the Department of Administration and Educational Leadership at The University of Alabama at Tuscaloosa. He has been a professor at Iowa State University and has held positions as a professor at Cleveland State University and Western Kentucky University and as an adjunct professor at the University of Michigan, Michigan State University, Eastern Michigan University, and Northern Michigan University. Herman has also had 20 years of experience as a school superintendent in districts in the states of Michigan and New York and as an assistant superintendent for instruction, elementary and secondary director, principal, research and developmental specialist, audiovisual coordinator, and teacher at the elementary, junior high, senior high, and junior college levels.

Herman received his B.S. degree from Northern Michigan University with concentrations in history, biology, and physical education. His M.A. and Ph.D. degrees in educational administration are from the University of Michigan.

Dr. Herman has done postdoctoral study in business administration at the University of Michigan and has acted as a consultant to school districts and to industry. He has authored 10 books, 15 monographs, and more than 150 articles on a wide range of educational and business issues. He has recently authored texts on strategic planning, human resource development, collective negotiations, and school-based management and is currently writing texts on school facilities and on total quality management in schools. He has received numerous professional honors and awards in the field of administration and educational leadership.

Janice L. Herman is an associate professor in the Department of Educational Leadership at The University of Alabama at Birmingham. She has been an assistant professor at the Department of Curriculum and Instruction at The University of Alabama at Tuscaloosa and was a Cooperative Superintendency Fellow in educational administration at The University of Texas at Austin. Her experience also includes work in school accreditation for the Texas state department of education, elementary school principalship with responsibility for instructional supervision in bilingual and English as a Second Language programs, and teaching in grades kindergarten through six and in gifted and talented education. She also taught in Thailand at the International School of Bangkok and at the American University Alumnae Association.

Dr. Herman received her B.A. from the College of William and Mary with a concentration in elementary education, an M.S. in education from the University of Southern California, and a Ph.D. in educational administration from The University of Texas at Austin. Dr. Herman has assisted in the preparation of the State of Texas instructional leadership model; has trained teachers, supervisors, administrators, and state department personnel in instructional leadership and effective teaching strategies; and has provided school improvement training for principals. Her consulting experience has been in the areas of school improvement and school-based management. She has recently authored texts on human resource development and school-based management and is currently writing a text on total quality management in schools.

1 How School Leaders Create Change

Chapter 1 provides an overview of the importance of administrators creating positive change in schools, school districts, and education. It presents several change theories, a change model, and various styles and theories of leadership. Being aware of the dynamics of change and knowing how to facilitate the change process are critical in effectively implementing an operational district or school plan.

Change Theories as Aids for Administrators

As with the married couple having their first child, which provides the opportunity to adjust to change and enrich the lives of all parties, or with the death of a beloved parent, which causes reflection upon one's own life and an opportunity to adjust one's life-style, change in our educational institutions is ever present and provides opportunities for positive growth.

Educational administrators, if they are to become true leaders, must take changes as positive challenges to improve the schools and the school districts of this nation. To lead, an effective leader must have followers and must also have developed a strong system of diverse leadership.

As educational leaders, it falls upon our shoulders to lead change in the direction we believe it should be headed. If we have developed a clear preferred future vision for our school or school district, and if we have a critical mass of stakeholders who claim ownership to that vision, we can utilize change opportunities to speed our journey toward that preferred future vision. This leadership quality is of utmost importance as we approach a new century. For we must again build confidence in and support for our schools.

It is the task and obligation of educational leaders to take advantage of the cries for change that exist today and use these cries as a challenge to mobilize the schools' resources to improve and attain the ultimate future vision.

Just review the current cries for change from legislators, business, parents, national research groups, and national political groups: An educational leader must lead the change—not merely be subject to it. Some of the current cries for change that are almost daily laid upon those in education include:

- We need better-trained workers in business and industry in order to become more competitive in the world market; and schools must do a better job.
- Our students compare very poorly to students of other nations on standardized test scores, especially in math and science; and our schools must improve this situation.
- Schools must increase their use of technology in order to improve.
- Schoolteachers and administrators must be held more accountable for the quality of the products they turn out; and tenure should be eliminated.
- Schools cannot undergo piecemeal patching; they must be totally restructured.
- Give students and parents a choice of which school and school district the students attend, and this will automatically identify the good schools and school districts and cause the poor ones to improve because of the attendant pressure of their public identification.

- Empower parents and community members and teachers to make many of the decisions that have historically been made by boards of education and superintendents of schools, and allow those decisions to be made at the school site level rather than at the central office level.

In order to react to these cries for change in our schools and lead stakeholders to improve education at the school building and school district levels, the administrators must possess a clear knowledge of change concepts and processes. At this point, let us explore the following: (1) the categories of organizational change in which schools may become involved, (2) priorities for successful management of transformational change, (3) means of determining the school's, school district's, or individual's readiness for change, (4) aids in overcoming resistance to change, (5) stages of an individual's resistance to change, and (6) actions that a leader can take to ensure that the change(s) will be positive in nature (Schlechty, 1990).

1. Categories of organizational change in which schools may become involved are of three types. The first type is one of *optional change*, which is the preferred type when key groups of employees initiate the change, rather than having the change mandated by the board of education, the superintendent of schools, or the school principal. The second type is *incremental change*, which is the preferred choice when the school's or school district's operations are working well, but the stakeholders agree that minor changes will improve the current operations to an even greater degree. The final type is identified as *transformational change*. This is the only rational choice to be made when a school or school district is working poorly, or when outside or inside forces are demanding radical changes in the way instructional, support services, or governance matters are being conducted. Transformational change is dramatic in structure and rapid in transition and it will ultimately radically change the entire culture of the organization.

2. Priorities for successful management of transformational change, if carefully considered prior to initiating change, can greatly

assist the leader in ensuring that the change will be successfully implemented. These priority conditions are keys to success:

- There must be a commitment to the change(s) by the leaders and by a critical mass of stakeholders.
- There should exist a clear, preferred future vision of what the school or school district will look like when the change is completed.
- There should exist clear-cut strategic goals that are to be reached as the organization undergoes the change process, and milestones should be established to guide the path of change.
- Detailed tactical plans must be decided upon and be made available in understandable language to all who are to participate in the change process.
- Training must be provided for those individuals who are to initiate and/or manage the change if they do not possess the prerequisite knowledge or skills that are necessary.
- Adequate time, finances, material, and human resources must be provided in order to enhance the probability of successful change taking place.
- High-quality, comprehensive, and frequent two-way communications must take place throughout the entire change process.
- Adjustments to the tactical or strategic plans must be made during the formative aspects of the change process if changes are required during the initiation and implementation stages of change.
- The leader should provide recognition for all who do good work and must attend group celebrations every time an important milestone is reached.

3. Determining the school's, school district's, or individual's readiness for change can be accomplished by answering a few simple guide questions, such as the following:

Does my school or school district have a clear vision of what should be or what could be in the future?

Does my school or school district have a clear picture of both what is currently in existence and the qualitative level of what exists?

Are inside forces or powerful outside sources clamoring for change?

Does my school or school district constantly try to improve, and do the leaders encourage all of us to present changes that may improve the school or school district?

Does my school or school district collect data on the results of its programs and determine the impacts of our efforts?

Does my school or school district look toward the future with a clear and positive vision, lay immediate and continuous plans to achieve this vision, and use the past and current accomplishments as baselines upon which to improve?

As an individual, do I share in the vision for my school or school district?

Do I enjoy new challenges and new ways of doing things, and am I willing to assist my school or school district in making positive changes?

Do I look forward to taking part in new learning and working opportunities?

Do I look toward the future, plan for it in the present, and use the past and present as baselines upon which to improve?

4. Assistance in overcoming resistance to change becomes very important when trying to initiate transactional change, because there will always be some employees or important stakeholders who will resist any suggested change. First, it is important to provide as much security as possible for those who will become involved in change, especially those who are reluctant to change. The leaders (principals, superintendents, and change agents) should provide detailed information about what will be changed and what will remain as it always has been. They should also provide statements to reinforce the security needs

of those who will be expected to initiate and maintain the desired change(s). Also, they should emphasize and widely communicate and sell, if you will, the expected positive benefits to be achieved for the school, the school district, the pupils, the employees, and the community as the change is implemented. Finally, the leaders should develop contingency plans to deal with the logical and emotional resistance of individuals and groups who form resistance to change.

5. Stages of an individual's resistance to change follow a specific pattern of stages, and leaders must be aware of and know how to isolate and deal with each of these stages. The stages of an individual's resistance to change are eight in number:

- Stage One: Denial
- Stage Two: Defensiveness
- Stage Three: Interest
- Stage Four: Involvement
- Stage Five: Acceptance
- Stage Seven: Internalization
- Stage Six: Adaptation
- Stage Eight: Ownership

6. Actions that a leader can take to help ensure that the change(s) will be positive in nature include the following:

- Unfreeze the current state to make sure change of some nature has to take place.
- Have key leaders and decision makers in the school or school district not only investigate why change must take place but also buy into this identified *need*. A need can be defined as a gap or discrepancy between "what should be" and "what is."
- Before initiating the change process, develop a critical mass of stakeholders who will support the need for change.
- Based upon the need for change being identified and supported, the leader can work to arrive at consensus on the specific goals and objectives required to change to the preferred future vision.
- Next, the leaders work with the stakeholders to develop specific tactical plans aimed at achieving the strategic goals and objectives to be accomplished.

- Finally, the leader must develop a data gathering and communication two-way feedback system throughout the change process so that all involved know what is happening, how well the plans are working, and at what stage of the change process the school or the school district has arrived (Herman, 1989e).

The section that follows describes several usable change models that can effectively translate into practice the theories just described.

Change Models as Aids for Administrators

Once the leaders have gathered a critical mass of supportive stakeholders and understand the crucial aspects of change as they relate to the organization and to the individuals who may be involved, they should develop a change model to guide the actions that will have to take place if transactional change is to result in success. An example of a change model is presented in Table 1.1.

This model should serve as a guide for managing the change process required for implementing the planning strategies described in this book. Since productive change demands an administrative climate of nurturance, it seems advisable to codify that process. Now that we have viewed a change model and discussed the special characteristics of change, let us turn to the types of leadership that exist in the wide variety of principals, superintendents, and other leaders in schools.

Autocratic Style of Leadership: Its Advantages and Disadvantages

Autocratic leaders many times resist change because they want to control every aspect of their organization. In all probability, this type of leadership can be effective only when there is an emergency condition existing that must be addressed without any dialogue with other stakeholders. Perhaps an unexpected wildcat strike by an employees' union or a serious disturbance by the

TABLE 1.1 A Vertical Stages Change Model

Current Stage: Maintenance of status quo

Stage One: Unfreezing the status quo (beginning renewal and change)

Stage Two: Awareness by individuals and/or the school or school district decision makers or stakeholders of the need for change

Stage Three: Acceptance of involvement by individuals and/or groups

Stage Four: Action planning, which involves determining "what is" and "what should be" and arriving at alternate routes to achieve what should be. Next, it involves selecting the best solutions from the alternatives and developing detailed tactical plans that respond to the questions: Why? When? Where? What? Who? and How?

Stage Five: Assessment and evaluation take place throughout the change process by collecting data, arraying data in an understandable and helpful manner, and analyzing the data as a basis for making operational decisions.

Stage Six: Decisions are made whether to modify the plans and try again or to implement the change because it has achieved the purposes it intended to achieve.

Stage Seven: Refreezing is important if the decision is that the change has achieved what it was intended to achieve. If the change is not refrozen and change is permitted to continue, the school or school district will not be able to stabilize the improvements that were effected by the planned change.

Stage Eight: Status quo is reestablished and the resulting changes become the normal operating procedures; those, in turn, become part of the new organizational culture of the school and/or the school district.

Stage Nine: Monitoring and scanning of external and internal key variables are done continuously to determine if and when there is a requirement to once again refreeze the organization and begin anew the change process.

students of a high school might be two of the few times that the autocratic style may be useful. Once the crisis is resolved, this type of leadership has served its purpose. An autocratic leader will probably never be able to cause positive long-term change in any school organization, whether it is an individual school or an entire school district. A sharply contrasting style follows.

Laissez-Faire Style of Leadership:
Its Advantages and Disadvantages

The laissez-faire style of leadership is so very weak that it amounts to no direction by the principal or superintendent who uses this style. The only time this leadership can be effective in implementing changes is when the leadership for change comes from teachers, other employees, or other stakeholders of the school or school district. The only advantage of this style, during a period of required change, is that this leader will not interfere with the work of others who are initiating and managing the change process. This leadership style will work when nonadministrators fill the void in leadership that is left by laissez-faire administrators. Like the autocratic style, however, it is not going to work over the long term.

A good example of this style is when the positional leader turns over all curriculum decisions to the faculty, and the leader does not monitor or judge the quality of those decisions on instructional programs. A more moderate and contemporary style follows.

Democratic Style of Leadership:
Its Advantages and Disadvantages

A democratic leader involves others in most decision-making situations. This is by far the preferred style for the long term. Others perceive the leader as being strong enough to permit broad input into decisions, and the faculty and other stakeholders gain ownership of the decisions. If you are a part-owner, you tend to want to make the decision work well. About the only time this style is not preferred is when the administrative leader has to make a quick decision in an emergency situation. If these quick decisions happen infrequently, the stakeholders will not complain, because they are normally involved and they understand the requirement of quick action during an emergency.

An excellent example of democratic leadership is that of involving teachers, classified employees, students, parents, and community members in long-term planning to determine the needs of the district. Once the needs (gaps between what is and what should be) are determined, this same group of stakeholders can play a large role in designing means to achieve the identified needs.

A more education-specific description of a leadership style follows.

Positional Leadership:
Its Advantages and Disadvantages

Positional leadership refers to those persons who have an official title, such as the building principal or the superintendent of schools. This type of leadership is provided by giving someone an official title that denotes a certain degree of power simply because of her or his position in the school building or the school district.

The main advantages of this type of leadership are: (a) It brings the full force of the organization's official structure to bear on the leader, and if structured properly, it brings both authority and an equal amount of accountability to the leader; and (b) it provides an official position from which the leader can grow and learn to provide other types of leadership that may be even more important.

The most clear disadvantage is that someone in this category of leadership can order other subordinates around but cannot order them to be happy, productive, or effective in their responsibilities. At its very worst, this type of leadership can lead to "snoopervision" and a dictatorial style, whereby others are treated almost like slaves who are to take care of every whim of the leader. A more classic leadership style description follows.

Referent Leadership:
Its Advantages and Disadvantages

Referent leadership refers to situations where the leader (principal, others) gains some leadership because of power persons he or she can utilize. For example, the superintendent may refer to the board of education, or the principal may refer to the superintendent of schools. Again, a curriculum specialist who is having trouble convincing a teachers' committee to adopt a certain category of curriculum may refer to the expert in curriculum from a university or to the author of that specific curricular content.

Referent leadership is used in an attempt to prove to others that one's suggestions are correct and are based on higher authority or on expertise. The downside is that if one uses it too frequently, it becomes a sign of weakness because the leader never promotes an issue on its own merits but rather uses others as a not-too-subtle way of gaining personal agenda items. A description of two similar styles follows.

Informational Leadership:
Its Advantages and Disadvantages

Informational leadership is always a valid part of leadership. Simply stated, leaders should have access to information that will assist them and others involved in decision making to make intelligent choices. Since, however, many hot issues are decided on an emotional basis, informational leadership may be insufficient, by itself, to cause the desired changes to take place.

Personal Leadership:
Its Advantages and Disadvantages

Personal leadership is a very desirable type. This category of leader gains followers because of what she or he is, not because of the official position as principal, superintendent, or some other official title. This type may be the result of a person's charisma, or a person who contains superior knowledge in many areas, or a person whom others love, or a person who involves others to such an extent and who is so honest and fair that everyone trusts the leader. Obviously, this leader possesses the tremendous advantage of having numerous believers who will follow because of the personal characteristics and operational procedures of this leader.

There are two potential disadvantages of this leadership style as it relates to the school or school district over a long period of time: (a) People may have so much faith and trust in this personal leader that they rarely ever question the leader; and (b) if this leader leaves the school or school district, many times things fall apart because the leadership role was too focused on one person.

More contemporary theories are described next.

Leadership Theories:
Contingency, Transactional, and Transformational

Before discussing the three terms *contingency, transactional,* and *transformational,* as they apply to leadership, we require a clear definition of the terms as they will be used during this discussion. The terms can be simply defined as follows:

- *Contingency* is a possibility that must be prepared against.
- *Transaction* is the management of any affair or business deal.
- *Transform* means to give a different form to something.

Contingency Leadership: As it applies to leadership, the contingency theory implies a leader who will make a wide variety of decisions based upon the conditions at the time of making those decisions. The variables, which exist and impact on the decision at the exact time it is made, will incline the leader to make the specific decision. If the variables that impact the decision change, the leader may well make a different decision.

An example might well be one in which a superintendent of schools wishes to close an old and deteriorating neighborhood elementary school, based on factual information about its inadequacy in providing an appropriate learning environment for children, its extremely high maintenance costs, and that it is only being used to 20% of its capacity. Once the superintendent's ideas are known to the community, there is an uproar from the parents and residents in the area. Upon contacting the board of education members and explaining that this area has always voted favorably on tax increases and bond issues for the school district, the board members apply pressure to the superintendent.

The result is that the superintendent decides to recommend a bond issue to remodel the school, rather than to close it. Economically, this is a very poor decision. Politically, and for future support of taxpayers, this may be a wise long-term decision. Had enormous pressure not been placed on the superintendent, she might very well have gone with her original recommendation, which would have not only saved millions of taxpayer dollars but also greatly improved the learning environment for the children (Keith & Girling, 1991).

Transactional Leadership: Transactional leadership is one in which there is a give-and-take relationship with others. This type of leader determines what she or he wishes to have or accomplish and decides what she or he can barter or give to powerful individuals or groups to support those wishes.

Two examples will clarify the operational style of these categories of leaders. First, a school principal wants the teachers to voluntarily provide parent-teacher conferences in the evening, because practically all families with children in the school either have both parents working or have a single parent in the home who works. Upon hearing of the principal's plan, the teachers' union files a grievance, indicating that it will advise the teachers to not comply, since they will not receive additional pay and this service is not part of the existing master contractual agreement between the union and the board of education.

Upon meeting with the union leadership and conferring with the superintendent of schools, all agree that this procedure would be well received by the community. However, some give-and-take had to take place before the union leadership would advise the teachers to participate. A deal was reached that allowed the teachers to take the equivalent amount of days off, one-half day at a time, because a substitute teacher would be hired to cover their classrooms during their absence.

The next example involves a conflict situation between an athletic director and the director of music. In this case, when figuring the schedules for the performance of the athletic teams and the musical performing groups, independent of one another, it was discovered that a basketball game was scheduled on the same day that the band was to participate in regional adjudications. Also, it was discovered that the county track meet was scheduled at the same time as the spring concert by the vocal music groups.

After much discussion, the athletic director agreed to reschedule the basketball game, and the director of music agreed to move the date of the spring vocal music concert. More importantly, the two directors reached two other agreements: (a) They would share their tentative schedules before they were finalized; and (b) in cases of unavoidable conflicts in schedules, students who participated in both sports and music would be free to make whichever choice they preferred, with no pressure being applied by coaches or music teachers.

Transformational Leadership: A transformational leader is one who empowers others and causes a transformation, or drastic and irreversible change, in the way business is conducted in the school building or the school district. By empowering stakeholders to make decisions, this leader broadens the leadership base and allows desired changes to take place because there is a broad ownership of those changes and the stakeholders are integrally involved in the decisions to make the changes (Hanson, 1991).

An excellent example of transformational leadership activity is one whereby a school district and the principals in that district voluntarily go to site-based management structures that involve numerous stakeholders, who previously had no official say in the decisions that were made, to make decisions related to their school. Decisions related to budget, instruction, personnel, and governance, when done on the basis of the individual school and on the basis of group decision making, transform the entire organizational culture of the individual schools and the school district.

Now that change has been discussed as it relates to administrators creating changes in the schools' operations, and the various categories of leadership have been discussed and examples provided, it will be helpful to create a checklist to assist in reviewing the major points of emphasis that were covered in this chapter.

Leadership Checklist

Directions: Place an X in each box that identifies your knowledge or style.

- ☐ I have a vision of what my school (school district) can and should be in the future.
- ☐ I know the difference among the terms *optional change, incremental change,* and *transformational change* and I understand when each type is most appropriate.
- ☐ I know how to determine an individual's and an organization's readiness for change.
- ☐ I fully realize the implications of the various stages of an individual's resistance to change.
- ☐ I know actions that I can take to ensure that changes will be positive.
- ☐ I can produce a change model that will assist me and the school's stakeholders in causing positive change.
- ☐ I am an autocratic leader.
- ☐ I am a laissez-faire leader.
- ☐ I am a democratic leader.
- ☐ I use a positional leadership style.
- ☐ I use a referent style of leadership.
- ☐ I use an informational leadership style.
- ☐ I use a personal leadership style.
- ☐ I am a believer in the contingency theory of leadership.
- ☐ I am a believer in transactional leadership.
- ☐ I am a believer in the use of the transformational style of leadership.

Reminders

1. Be sure of a commitment to change by leaders and stakeholders.
2. Keep priority conditions for successful management in mind.
3. Develop a change model to guide actions.
4. Consider leadership styles and interactions when implementing change.

Summary

Chapter 1 provided an overview of the importance of administrators in causing positive change in schools, noting that in order
to react to demands for change in our schools, and in order to lead
stakeholders to improve education at the school building and
school district levels, the administrators must possess a clear
knowledge of change concepts and processes. Categories of organizational change were described: *optional change*, which is the
preferred type when key groups of employees initiate the change;
incremental change, which is the preferred choice when the school's
or school district's operations are working well; and *transformational change*, which will change the entire culture of the organization. Priority conditions for successful transformational change
were provided, as were the means of determining the school's or
district's readiness for change, a description of how to overcome
resistance to change, the stages of that resistance, and appropriate
actions to ensure change.

A sample change model and a discussion of various types of
leadership styles and theories preceded a concluding leadership
checklist that reviewed the chapter's major points of emphasis.

2 Blueprint for Leadership

LONG-TERM PLANNING

Chapter 2 defines long-term or strategic planning, presents a strategic planning model for use by administrators, and provides an overview of the various steps involved in strategic planning. Examples for each of the strategic planning steps clarify their execution. Linkages exist between strategic and tactical planning, which are defined by the operationalizing of the former by the latter. The chapter's thrust is to demonstrate these linkages as they are actually used by administrators in schools and school districts.

Definition of Strategic Planning

Strategic planning is long-term planning to achieve a preferred future vision for an organization, school, or school district. It defines the *whats* to be achieved. Once the strategic plans are completed, those plans are turned over to the tactical planners (Ryans & Shanklin, 1985). *Tactical planning* refers to the planning elements related to the *hows*. In other words, strategic planning spells out what is to be achieved to obtain the preferred future vision, while tactical planning spells out the detail work to be successfully completed to obtain the strategic goals spelled out during the strategic planning stage.

A Strategic Planning Model

Now that we have defined strategic planning, let us investigate a strategic planning model. Such a model is presented in Figure 2.1.

Step #1 in the model is that of the leader and/or the leader and stakeholders reaching consensus of a *vision of what should be* for the school or school district at some point in the future. To avoid the problem of collecting too much data and inhibiting the process prior to reaching consensus on Vision #1, it is best to have the persons involved create a vision on the basis of their individual visions. Next, as they share their individual visions, they can reach a consensus on the tentative vision for the school district. This process will be repeated later after much data is collected and analyzed to form the operating Vision #2.

While discussing and reaching consensus on this vision, the planning stakeholders should consider the role of the school or school district in the *mega* (societal), *macro* (total school district), and *micro* (school building) environments. Each of these important environments must be included in the preferred future vision for there to be a truly comprehensive strategic plan of what should be at some future time (Kaufman & Herman, 1989).

Step #1A is a very important point in arriving at information that will assist in reaching consensus on Vision #2. The *beliefs and visions* held by the stakeholders, relating to students, parents, community, instructional and co-curricular programs, governance, and many other matters that express their values and beliefs, should be incorporated into the operating vision. This stage may take a considerable period of time since any group will probably vary in the types and number of beliefs and values held by individual members of the group. Eventually, a consensus will be achieved on those core beliefs and values that must be incorporated into the preferred future vision for the school or school district (Herman, 1989a).

Step #1B identifies the task of completing an *external scanning* of variables that may impact the preferred future vision. Some examples of such external forces include actions by legislative bodies, actions by courts, money to finance the district, plans for either expansion or downsizing by businesses in the area, and any

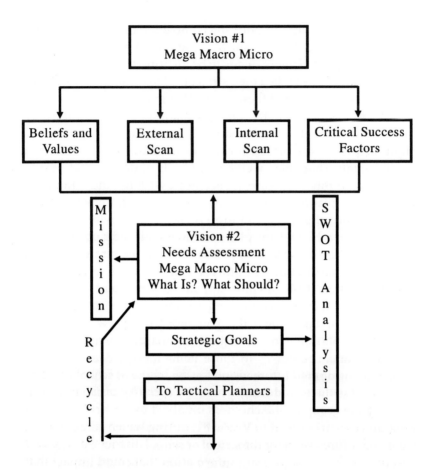

Figure 2.1. Strategic Planning Model

other force outside the district or school that might impact the strategic plans to achieve the preferred future vision. Once the data are collected for a reasonable number of years, trends can appear. These trends will allow the strategic planners to formulate means of dealing with these trends as the plans become operative.

Step #1C identifies the task of *internal scanning*. At this step, data are collected on variables, internal to the school or school district, which may impact the strategic plans. Some variables for which data should be collected will be normative-and-criterion referenced test results, dropout and completion rates, and measures of school climate. Collecting data on these variables over a reasonable number of years will allow trends to be identified and analyzed. The planners can then establish their strategic plans with full knowledge of the potential impact of these trends (Herman, 1989a).

Step #1D is crucial in the strategic planning process. It is a step in which the stakeholders must reach consensus on which six to eight factors are the most critical ones in achieving their desired future vision. There may well be hundreds of desires that people would like. If this is the case, it becomes a wish list and it impedes the strategic planning process. By identifying those six to eight characteristics that they feel are crucial if the preferred future vision is to be achieved, the planners have achieved a position that will greatly assist those who are to manage the strategic plans. Some of the major benefits of identifying the six to eight Critical Success Factors (CSF) include: (a) identifying clear directional priorities; (b) focusing continuing communication, data gathering, analysis, and decision making on the relatively few CSF; and (c) directing the allocation of the majority of financial, temporal, material, and human resources to those items identified as critical in achieving the desired future vision for the school or school district.

Step #2 is the step during which the *operating vision* is agreed upon by the group of stakeholders involved in the strategic planning process. In contrast to Vision #1, during which consensus on a desired future vision for the school or school district was reached absent any data or significant information that could impact that desired future vision, Vision #2 can be identified with a much more knowledgeable overview of the potential future. Before creating Vision #2, the planners will have at hand: (a) a consensus beliefs and values statement, (b) variable and trends that will impact the school or school district from the external environment, (c) variables and trends that will impact the school or school district from the internal environment, and (d) consensus on those six to eight factors that the group of planners agree are critical if the preferred vision is to be achieved at some point in the future.

Once all of these matters are considered, an operating vision, based on a variety of important information, can be reached. This stage should also be the stage where the needs can be identified.

A *need* may be defined as a gap or discrepancy between "what is" and "what should be." The task of what is has been primarily done by scanning the internal and external environments for impacting trends. The "what should be" is completed when the planners reach consensus of the preferred future Vision #2. Identification of needs is an important pre-step to developing the strategic goals for what should be at some future time.

Step #3 is that of creating a one-sentence statement of *mission* that will define the primary focus of the school or the school district. This mission statement should be derived from Vision #2, but it should also be spelled out in clear language so it can be used as the marketing rallying cry for the employees, the students, and the entire school community.

Step #4 involves the establishment of *strategic goals*. These goals are derived from the vision and mission statement and are the guidelines that indicate in detail what is to be achieved at some point in the future. These *whats* will allow the tactical planners to devise the *hows* (the detailed plans) to achieve the strategic goals. As is true of the vision statement, the strategic goals should be derived from the school's or school district's role(s) related to the mega (societal), macro (total school district), and micro (school building) environments.

Step #4A is the final step in the strategic planning exercise, the one at which the stakeholders who have created the vision, mission, and strategic goals turn the planning detail over to the operational people within the school or the school district. This final step involves conducting a Strengths, Weaknesses, Opportunities, and Threats (SWOT) analysis of both the external environmental factors and the internal environmental factors.

Once the *strengths* within and without the school or school district have been identified, the planners can devise ways to build upon those strengths and also find ways to utilize them in a positive manner to achieve the preferred future vision. An internal example could well be the support of many students through community booster groups. An external example could be that each school has entered a partnership with a business or industry in the community.

Once the *weaknesses* within and without the school or school district are identified, the planners can create ways of overcoming the identified weaknesses. An internal weakness might be that too many students drop out prior to graduation. An external weakness might be that some powerful local taxpayer group always lobbies against raising required taxes.

Upon identifying the *opportunities* that exist in the internal and external environments, the planners can devise means of capitalizing on those opportunities. An internal example might be that the classified employees (even though most live in the school district) have never, or very seldom, been asked to participate with the teachers and administrators in any planning or in selling the district and its programs to the community. An external opportunity might exist where there are many retired persons who could be used as tutors for children having difficulty with reading, science, or math.

Upon identifying the *threats* that exist in the internal and external environments, the planners can devise schemes to eliminate or at least lessen the degree of impact that the threats will have on the school or the school district. An external example could well be that the local governmental officials are publicly criticizing the schools. An internal example could be that the teachers' union is contemplating going on strike, which will negatively affect community support.

It must be emphasized that the tactical plans to deal with the SWOTs are to be left to the planners, who will be responsible for devising and managing the tactical plans to achieve the preferred future vision for the school or school district. However, it is the strategic planners who should identify the external and internal SWOTs to be dealt with by the tactical planners (Kaufman & Herman, 1991a). The next step is that of activating the tactical planning and recycling process.

Tactical Planning and Recycling

Once the strategic planners have completed their work of (a) reaching consensus on a preferred future vision, (b) devising a mission statement, (c) establishing strategic goals, and (d) completing a SWOT analysis, they should turn all of their work over to the tactical planners. The tactical planners shall then devise detailed plans designed to achieve the strategic goals and the school's or district's preferred future vision. Tactical planning will be discussed in detail in Chapter 3.

Even though the work of the strategic planners is turned over to the tactical planners, three activities still have to be conducted by those responsible for the oversight of the strategic plan. *First,* occasionally the stakeholders should be called back together to review the beliefs and values statement to determine whether changes should be made and how these changes might affect the preferred future vision for the school or school district. *Second,* the internal and external scans should be consistently conducted to determine whether new important impacting variables and/or trends have appeared on the scene and how these new variables will be dealt with in the strategic plan. *Third,* a SWOT analysis should be conducted periodically to determine whether any of these items, internally or externally, have changed and how these changes could effect the strategic plan.

Finally, it is important that those responsible for strategic planning periodically report back to all stakeholders regarding the status of the strategic plan. Although the stakeholders will have initial ownership of the plan they assisted in developing, they will soon lose support for the schools and faith in the administrative leadership if they are not consulted on a regular basis (Gilmore & Lozier, 1987).

Now that the strategic planning model has been presented, it will be elaborated upon by relating a short example of the steps in the model when it is used by a local school district.

A School District Example of a Strategic Plan

Wonderful School District involved a wide variety of stakeholders in their strategic planning process. Below is an abbreviated listing of the results achieved by this strategic planning process.

Vision #1: The stakeholders' strategic planning group for the Wonderful School District included the following components in their first vision, which was developed without any data collection prior to establishment of this tentative vision.

- Students, parents, and community members ought to be treated as valued customers by the employees of the district.
- Employees also ought to treat each other as valued customers.
- High standards of achievement should be held for students and employees.
- The schools should produce productive citizens upon graduation; that is, the schools should turn out students who produce more than they consume.
- The school environment should be one that is safe, healthy, and caring.
- The schools should be responsible for high-quality products and services.
- The schools should join with business, industry, health services, recreation services, and other groups to provide integrated and comprehensive human services to students whenever feasible.
- The schools have a responsibility to lead the community when it comes to identified needs related to the welfare of students, but the schools should follow the community whenever other non-school organizations contribute services to the welfare of students. By collaborative actions, school people can both lead and serve; and this approach will be in the best interest of the students, the schools, and the community as a whole.

Beliefs and values were decided upon after reaching consensus of Vision #1, and they included some of the same thoughts that appeared during the visioning process. However, a few additional ones were identified, which included the following:

- All students can learn.
- A comprehensive curriculum should be offered students because they will differ in their interests and in their future endeavors.

- Students should value their teachers, and teachers should value each of their students.
- Student achievement should be carefully monitored, and high achievement by students should be both the goal and the focal point of the schools.
- School climate should be both nurturing and demanding of results.
- Parents, community members, employees, and students all have appropriate roles to play in a collaborative decision-making structure.
- Schools must be operated in an efficient and effective manner, within the financial resources provided by the federal, state, and local governments and by the funds provided by the local taxpaying public.

External scanning by the Wonderful School District's strategic planners indicates that demographic, political, social, and economic factors are all important variables to be scanned. Such matters as the following were included in the scanning activities:

- Business and industry future plans
- Community attitude toward schools
- Legislation from federal, state, and local governmental units that have an impact on the schools
- Court decisions that have an impact on schools
- Shifts in population related to age, race, and socioeconomic level that will have an impact on schools
- Trends in such matters as private school enrollments and parental choice

Internal scanning by the Wonderful School District's strategic planners revealed the following trends:

- A great increase in single-parent homes and homes where both parents work
- A decline in parent and community attendance at school-sponsored activities

- A lessening of financial support at the state level
- A more adversarial union/management environment that seems to be evolving
- An increase in the percentage of students who drop out of school

Critical Success Factors (CSF) to which the strategic planners agreed included: (1) a high level of student achievement; (2) a high level of community support; (3) a reasonable level of financial support from all fiscal sources; (4) highly skilled teachers and administrators; (5) interaction, collaborative planning, and two-way communication with other governmental agencies, businesses, health and recreation agencies, and other groups that also have an interest in human services; and (6) a climate that is caring, open, demanding of high achievement, and respectful of all parties.

Vision #2 was a modification of Vision #1, based upon (a) the beliefs and values of the stakeholders, (b) the trends revealed by internal and external scanning, and (c) the list of the six CSF.

A mission statement was developed out of Vision #2, a single-sentence mission with some supplemental points of elaboration added to make the mission even clearer for communication purposes. The mission statement adopted by consensus of the strategic planners for Wonderful School District was:

The mission of Wonderful School District is to develop well-educated and productive graduates and enable the teachers and other employees of the school district to accomplish this in a caring and demanding manner.

Measures of how well this mission is accomplished include: (1) high student achievement scores; (2) low student dropout rates; (3) high student school attendance; (4) the number of students' receiving honors and scholarships to colleges and universities; (5) a school climate that makes the students and all who come in contact with the schools feel welcome, respected, and cared for; (6) positive attitudes about the students and support of the schools by the community; and (7) follow-up studies that indicate that the great majority of graduates are successful and productive citizens.

SWOT analyses reveal that the following strengths, weaknesses, opportunities, and threats exist. Both the external and internal environments were analyzed by the strategic planning committee. The findings are abbreviated below, and both the internal and external findings are combined for the sake of brevity.

The *strengths* that were revealed include: (a) a positive community attitude toward the schools; (b) union/management relations that are collaborative and positive in nature; (c) schools possessing a highly skilled teaching, classified, and administrative group of employees, with low employee turnover; and (d) an excellent fund balance in the district, which ensures fiscal stability.

The *weaknesses* include: (a) schools that have not kept up with state-of-the-art technology; (b) declining numbers in the student population, which could lessen the number of instructional offerings that can be offered students at a reasonable cost; and (c) some businesses in the school district that intend to close down, which could have a serious effect on employment opportunities and the financial tax base for the schools.

The *opportunities* that were currently untapped and were discovered through the SWOT analyses included: (a) organized retired groups in the community who have offered to serve as tutors for the elementary students and role models for at-risk students; and (b) businesses in the district that have decided to adopt schools, allowing teachers and administrators to attend their training activities without cost to the school district, and allowing students to shadow employees as a career option.

The *threats* that were discovered included: (a) the organization of a formal anti-tax group in the district; (b) financial difficulties at the largest industrial firm in the district; and (c) an outward migration to newer suburbs, which will likely cause the demographics of the community to undergo a dramatic change within the next 5 years.

Strategic goals became the final task of the strategic planning committee before it turned its information over to a tactical planning group. The strategic planning committee of the Wonderful School District passed on to the tactical planning committee a series of strategic goals. A few of these strategic goals are listed below. It must be emphasized, however, that strategic goals are the *whats* to be achieved, and the details are left to the tactical planners.

- Lower the student dropout rate
- Increase collaboration and/or partnership with the other organizations within the community
- Increase the school climate scores
- Provide for the students at risk
- Increase the investment earnings of the district
- Prove that all students are learning
- Increase the enrollments in math, science, and foreign languages (Kaufman & Herman, 1991b)

Now that we have defined strategic planning, presented a model of a strategic plan, and provided an abbreviated example of how the strategic planning model could operate in a local school district, it is still important to reemphasize some major points related to strategic planning.

Planning Stakeholders

A board of education, superintendent of schools, and/or an administrative staff can come up with a strategic plan. Even though the board and management employees are crucial supporters of strategic planning, and even though they may initiate the planning process, it will have very limited success if a critical mass of stakeholders do not buy into the plan. The best way to get stakeholders (teachers, classified employees, parents, students, community representatives, and administrators) to claim ownership of the strategic plans is to involve a broadly representative group in the activities of the planning process, particularly in the determination of needs.

Needs Assessment (Mega, Macro, and Micro)

A need is a gap or a discrepancy between the *desired future state* for the school or the school district and the *current state* that exists.

It is important for the school district's strategic planners to realize that the schools have certain societal roles that they play as an institution, and that some of these roles must be played in collaboration with other organizations.

It is also important when determining needs that all three dimensions of needs are examined by the strategic planners. In other words, the mega (societal) needs, the macro (total school district) needs, and the micro (individual school building) needs are all examined as a database for strategic planning. To either eliminate or miss any of these three categories is to have an incomplete strategic plan, and it will also probably diminish the chances of ultimately achieving the preferred future vision for the school or school district.

Likewise, essential to the achievement of that preferred future vision is the identification of the CSF.

Critical Success Factors (CSF)

The identification of CSF by the strategic planning committee is another crucial activity of the strategic planning process. These six to eight most highly important items must be identified and brought into the planning process as the primary foci of planning. That is, if it is critical for successful strategic outcomes to be achieved, it is critical that these CSF receive the greatest amount of attention; are given the largest portion of available resources; and become the foci of communication, data collection, and evaluation. A similar role is played by the development of a set of beliefs and values.

Beliefs and Values

It matters not what beliefs and values are held by the individuals involved in strategic planning, but it greatly matters that these beliefs are vocalized, discussed, and defended. Eventually, a consensus of beliefs and values should be placed in writing to assist in guiding the further stages of the strategic planning process. This process is followed by consideration of the impact of two environments.

External and Internal Scanning

Many external and internal variables may impact what goes on in schools and ought to be systematically investigated. Through the collection of data about the variables, which over time can lead to trends, the strategic planners can determine directionality and plan for the variables and their impact on the school or the school district.

Alternate and Preferred Futures

While scanning the external and internal variables, the strategic planners can develop a variety of hypothetical future scenarios. These alternate futures will be based upon determining the impact on the school or school district of the various trend lines. With the alternate scenarios available and with the potential impact on the school or school district assumed, the preferred future vision can be assembled and work begun to develop the strategic goals designed to be provided to the tactical planners who will develop action plans to achieve the strategic goals.

SWOT

Once the strategic planning group has developed its preferred future vision for the school or school district, it should undertake the task of analyzing the strengths, weaknesses, opportunities, and threats that exist in the internal school district's environment. The strategic planners should also conduct a SWOT analysis of the external environment. Together, the analyses will help the strategic and tactical planners take advantage of the strengths and opportunities available and will alert the strategic and tactical planners to the weaknesses that must be overcome and the threats that must be acted upon in a manner that either eliminates them or decreases their negative impact on the school or the school district.

Linkages to Tactical Planning

Finally, it must be stressed that once the initial work of the strategic planning committee is completed, the strategic planners must turn over their work to the tactical planners, who will devise and implement the specific operational plans designed to achieve the strategic goals. Remember that the strategic goals are the directional *whats*, while the tactical plans spell out the *hows* (Herman, 1989b).

Up to this point, strategic planning has been defined, a model has been presented, an example has been provided, and some major points have been given added emphasis. At this juncture, it will be helpful to develop a checklist for strategic planning.

Strategic Planning Checklist

Directions: Place an X in each box as you complete the steps indicated.

- ☐ A stakeholders' committee has been organized to assist in the strategic planning process.
- ☐ An initial vision for the school district has been spelled out, and consensus has been reached on it.
- ☐ A good amount of time has been expended on all members of the strategic planning committee telling the group about the actual beliefs and values related to schools. Eventually, the group achieved consensus upon which beliefs and values would be used to guide the remainder of the strategic planning process.
- ☐ External and internal variables were scanned to determine trends that may impact the schools.
- ☐ Those six to eight factors that were considered most critical to the success of the schools were identified and became the primary foci of the strategic planners.
- ☐ Needs were defined as gaps between what exists and the "what should be" vision for the schools. These needs were of the mega (societal) type, macro (total school district) type, and micro (individual school building) type.
- ☐ A final preferred future vision for the school or school district was developed.
- ☐ A SWOT analysis was completed on both the external and internal environment; and the information was utilized to

capitalize on the strengths, take advantage of the opportunities, plan to correct the weaknesses, and decide upon means to either eliminate or lessen the negative impact of the threats.

☐ The work of the strategic planners has been turned over to the tactical planning group. Remember that strategic planning deals with the *whats*, and tactical planning deals with the detailed *hows*.

☐ Individuals were named to continually monitor the external and internal environments. They are also to conduct periodic SWOTs and periodically call back the strategic planners to see if the beliefs and values have changed or to determine if the CSF have changed.

Reminders

1. Reach consensus on a vision, mission, and strategic goal selection.
2. Keep stakeholders updated on the status of the strategic plan.
3. Involve a broadly representative group in the planning process.
4. Obtain needs assessment data from all three dimensions: mega, macro, and micro.

Summary

Chapter 2 defined strategic planning as long-term planning to achieve a preferred future vision for an organization, school, or school district. The strategic planning model steps of visioning, creating beliefs, external and internal scanning, identification of the CSF, creation of an operating vision, identification of needs, establishment of mission and strategic goals, execution of an analysis of strengths, weaknesses, opportunities, and threats were described.

Examples for each of the strategic planning steps were provided. Some further major points that were emphasized were the involvement of planning stakeholders and the examination of the mega (societal), macro (total school district), and micro (individual school building) needs. The linkage to tactical planning and a strategic planning checklist concluded the chapter.

Building Blocks of Change

SHORT-TERM PLANNING AND

CONSENSUS BUILDING

Chapter 3 provides information about tactical planning and its uses by administrators. There are planning roles to be played during tactical planning by boards of education, superintendents, central office administrators, building principals and their assistants, teachers, classified employees, students, parents, and community members. Since common agreement among these stakeholders about the outcomes of school planning is essential, a variety of consensus-building techniques is included. This chapter also emphasizes the requirement for staff development and training activities for those individuals who will become involved in tactical planning activities.

A definition and model of tactical planning precedes the description of stakeholder roles, consensus building, and training requirements.

Tactical Planning Defined

Tactical planning is planning the detailed *hows* to achieve the *whats* (strategic goals) developed by the strategic planning committee (Carlson & Awkerman, 1991). An example will clarify this definition.

Strategic Goal: to provide a program to focus on children at risk.

Specific Objective: by the year 19—, the school district will have in place a comprehensive program focused on children at risk, and by that date the achievement levels of at-risk children will mirror the achievement levels of the general student population.

The Action Plan will provide specific answers to Why? Who? When? What? and How measured?

Tactical Planning Model

Once the strategic plan is provided to the tactical planners, those responsible for tactical planning would do well to provide the tactical planning committee with a model to follow while completing their work. Such a tactical planning model is displayed in Figure 3.1. The tactical planners follow this sequence in their planning operations.

1. Specific Objectives

First, they develop specific objectives for each strategic goal that has been developed. These objectives indicate the means to achieve the objectives and the means of measurement to be used at the agreed-upon time to determine whether the objective was achieved to a satisfactory degree.

2. Decision Rules

Second, they agree upon a set of decision rules they will use to determine which objective should be given priority attention, in case there are too many objectives to manage at one time. These decision rules, upon which consensus must be reached, should be of the commonsense variety. Some suggested decision rules include the following:

- The objective must be *achievable* and not related to an unreasonable wish list.

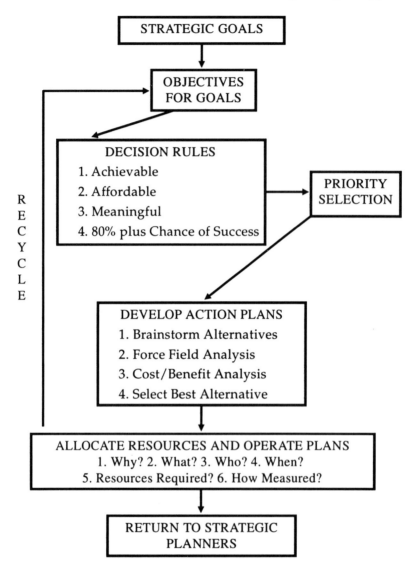

Figure 3.1. Tactical Planning Model

- The objective should be *affordable*, in the sense that it should not take financial, material, and human resources away from something that already exists that is of greater value.

- The objective should be *meaningful*.
- The initial objective should have an *80% plus chance* of being successfully completed.

As the management of the tactical plans takes place with a comprehensive planning group whose members have not previously worked together, it is important to initially select those objectives that have a very high probability of being successfully completed. If the initial objectives are too difficult and the attempt ends in failure, the committee will become demoralized. However, after the initial high probability objectives are successfully achieved and the tactical planning committee members become confident of their abilities to achieve the desired objectives, a much lower percentage (50% or less) of potential success objectives may and should be attempted.

3. Action Plans

Once the objectives are prioritized, using the decision rules that were agreed upon, the tactical planners can turn their attention to developing specific *action plans*. Since there may be more than one type of action plan considered to achieve the specific objective, it is wise not to prematurely select one plan before exploring all the possibilities. At this juncture, the tactical planners should undertake four activities (Herman, 1990a).

4. Brainstorming

The first activity to be undertaken is that of *brainstorming* potential actions. The desired outcome of the brainstorming exercise is to obtain as many ideas as possible in the shortest period of time (usually 10 to 15 minutes). To achieve this outcome, specific brainstorming rules should be carefully followed as a means of encouraging total participation and getting the greatest number of potential solutions suggested. The brainstorming rules should be similar to the following:

- All suggestions are welcomed and considered valid.
- Piggybacking (adding to) someone else's suggestion is permitted.

- Creative and innovative suggestions are encouraged.
- The person making the suggestion should not discuss or defend her or his suggestion at this time.
- *No comments or nonverbal actions indicating approval or disapproval of the suggestion are permitted.* If someone receives a disapproving statement or glance from another person involved in the brainstorming activity, that person either will withdraw from making additional suggestions or will break the rules by arguing with the person making the negative comment. Brainstorming works best when: (a) there are one or two recorders, (b) the participants practice obeying the rules before dealing with serious objectives, and (c) someone monitors and corrects violations of the rules (Bryson, 1988).

Following the brief brainstorming period, it is legitimate for the tactical planners to ask questions, to seek additional information, and to eliminate the suggestions that they feel are not relevant.

5. *Force Field Analysis*

Once the brainstorming is completed, the tactical planners turn to the activity of *force field analysis*. Force field analysis consists of taking each suggested action plan and determining which forces will probably be supportive of the suggestion and which will be constraining. Once the force field analysis is completed, the planners may again wish to collect data to determine the accuracy of their initial force field analysis. Let us look at an example of a school district that is considering starting a day-care program for preschool children whose parents both work or who live in a single-parent home.

Suggested Program: to create a public day-care program for working parents.

Force Field Analysis: An Example

Supporting Factors	Constraining Factors
parents	commercial day school
child welfare agencies	operators
business community	cost to the school district
other?	teachers

It may also be important to conduct a *cost/benefit analysis* of each suggested action. This procedure involves determining the value of what is achieved by the cost of carrying out the proposed action(s). If the ratio is favorable in terms of benefits, the program should be put into operation. If the program ratio is unfavorable in terms of cost, the program should not be initiated, and the planners should go back to the drawing board to create new suggestions.

Finally, after completing the brainstorming, conducting a force field analysis, and completing a cost/benefit analysis, the planners are ready to *select the best alternative* from all the alternatives offered. The planners are now ready to determine the specific responsibilities by allocating resources and carefully spelling out operating plans.

6. Tactical Planning Table

The allocation of resources and the careful defining of details of the operating plan for each best alternative selected to achieve the specific objective can best be completed by using a planning table.

Sample Tactical Planning Table

- Why?
- Who?
- What?

- When?
- Resources Required?
- How Measured?

Directions: Answer all of the above questions before initiating any program or action. Use the following examples to assist you in completing your Tactical Planning Table.

Program Considered: Starting a school district-sponsored day-care program for preschool youngsters who live within the school district.

Why? This program is being considered for two reasons: (1) There are many families in which both parents work, and there are other situations when children are left with a babysitter in homes in which there is a single parent, and the quality of child care is suspect in many cases. It also may be too expensive for some parents to handle. (2) It is believed that instructional programs can be created, as a pre-Headstart approach that will help these children be better prepared when they enter school at the kindergarten level.

Who? At this stage, a specific individual or group is designated to carry out each task. Using two of the examples from the tasks listed above will illustrate this point.

1. Survey potential clients—principals in each building under direction of the school/community relations director.
2. Review building capacity—the director of buildings and grounds.

What? This category indicates the detailed tasks to be completed to initiate, maintain, monitor, and evaluate the suggested program. It is best to develop a list of tasks to be completed before setting them in chronological order, because initially trying to establish chronological order will greatly slow down the planning process. An abbreviated example will clarify this point.

Task to Be Completed	Chronology of Completion
review building capacities	2
survey potential clients	1
develop time schedule for children's attendance	3
develop cost estimates	5
develop instructional program	4
others	6

When? In this case it was determined that there was a year-round need and that the target starting date would be the summer of 19—.

Resources Required? Once the what question is answered and the when is determined, the financial, temporal, and material resources can be allocated to each step in the planning process and to the operational phase of the program. For example, the survey of clients three times per year may be computed to cost $1,200 yearly.

How Measured? The planners determined that there would be three types of measurement applied to this program and that measurements would be taken at the end of the summer, the end of the fall, and the end of the spring. The three types of measurement agreed upon were: (1) an attitude survey of client satisfaction would indicate that a minimum of 95% would agree that they are completely satisfied with the program, (2) the program will come in on time and at or under budgeted costs, and (3) as students enter regular school, the teachers will judge them to be more ready than a control group of students who never attended the school district's day-care program.

Once all the action plans are completed, there is still a need for someone or some group to be responsible for *monitoring* each of the action programs. As each program is monitored and data are collected upon which to make decisions, the monitors may find that (a) the program is not working and should be eliminated, (b) the program requires some modifications and should be retained, or (c) the program is working well and requires no adjustments. If the program is not working, the planners must return to the step of setting objectives. If the program requires some modifications, the planners return to the step of developing action plans or to the step of allocating resources and developing detailed operational plans.

Also, the data collected and the decisions reached must be fed back to those who hold responsibility for strategic planning, because the strategic and tactical plans have to work in tandem to be effective. As changes are made in the strategic plans (the whats), these changes must immediately and clearly be communicated to the tactical planners. On the other hand, as changes are made in the tactical plans or as the monitoring results indicate problems, these problems and changes must also be immediately and clearly communicated to the strategic planners.

Establishing Strategic Goals

At this juncture, an example of the tactical planning process for a single strategic goal selected by the strategic planning committee and passed on to the tactical planners will illustrate each step in the tactical planning process.

Sample Tactical Planning Model

For this purpose we will assume that the school district's strategic planners passed on the following goal:

Strategic Goal: The schools are to become more involved in collaborative efforts with businesses, industries, civic groups, other governmental agencies, and other community organizations housed in the school district whenever the human services to students can be enhanced by collaborative and cooperative efforts.

Objectives:
1. Within 6 months of this date of March 1, 19—, to initiate a community planning committee, involving all groups who deal with the human needs of children.
2. By September 1, 19—, to have in place a cooperative health screening clinic in each school, managed by physicians and nurses from area hospitals and the school district's chief nurse.
3. By June 1, 19—, to have in place a joint summer program for the school children, cooperatively sponsored and operated by the city recreation department and the school district.

Decision Rules: By using the decision rules of: (1) achievable, (2) affordable, (3) meaningful, and (4) an 80% plus chance of success, the strategic planners decided to first tackle the first objective: to initiate a community planning committee, involving all groups who deal with the human needs of children.

Action Plans: The action planning begins with the brainstorming of alternative ways of achieving the objective. A few of the brainstorming suggestions given were: (a) get the community power figures to organize the Children's Human Needs Planning Committee, (b) ask the clergy to organize such a committee, (c) ask the law enforcement agency to organize such a committee, and (d) ask business and industrial corporations' CEOs to organize the committee.

Next a force field analysis (Kaufman & Herman, 1991b) was conducted for each of the suggestions. Two of these will serve as an example.

Force Field Analysis for Business and
Industrial CEOs to Organize the Committee (Example)

Supporting Forces	Constraining Forces
CEOs support the effort	Some parents are concerned about corporate control
Clergy support the effort	
School board supports the effort	Some health providers are concerned about loss of income
Most parents support the effort	Others
Others?	

Force Field Analysis for School District
Organizing the Committee (Example)

Supporting Forces	Constraining Forces
School board supports the effort	Some health providers do not support
CEOs support the effort	Private schools do not support
All parents support the effort	Fundamental religious groups do not support
Clergy supports the effort	
Other?	Some organizations were concerned about a power grab by school officials
	Other?

Once the force field was completed a cost/benefit analysis was conducted for each approach. It was determined that the cost/

benefit ratio would be favorable, regardless of which group sponsored the committee.

It was decided that the *best alternative* was to have the school be the chief sponsor of the committee. This phase of tactical planning completed, the planners turned to the detailed answers to the questions of Why? What? Who? When? Resources Required? and How Measured?

Why? This was the belief that a coordinated effort by all the community agencies interested in students' welfare could provide more effective and efficient student welfare service if they collaboratively and cooperatively teamed their efforts.

What? This involved all the detailed planning tasks required to make this a reality. Such details as who shall call the first meeting, how will an agenda be agreed upon, where will the meetings be held, what shall be the ultimate committee membership, and many other details would have to be decided upon and a chronological order of task completion would have to be developed.

Who? For each task listed, an individual or group who holds responsibility for completing that task is clearly identified.

When? This has been tentatively decided by the objective of having the committee in operation by March 1, 19—.

Resources Required? This stage of planning would require decisions as to the use of building space, secretarial assistance, the members of each group's time, materials needed to market the service, and many other details.

How Measured? Measurement would ultimately involve these matters:

1. Was the program operational by the March 1, 19— date? (this is the initial objective). Later, however, two other measures must be addressed:

2. Were the services provided to students of higher quality and/or less costly than the previous services provided by the independent agencies?

3. Were the students and their parents and/or guardians pleased with the services provided?

Monitoring of all action plans must take place to determine if they are working well. Data have to be collected and analyzed, and the decision must be made if the program is to be dropped or modified. This information must be systematically fed back to the tactical planners so they can take appropriate follow-up actions. This information must also be shared with those in charge of strategic planning, because both the tactical and strategic plans have to work in tandem to be of maximum effectiveness.

Now that we have (a) defined tactical planning, (b) presented a tactical planning model, and (c) provided an example of how the tactical planning model would work within a school district, it is time to turn to other matters that are important to consider when working in a planning process with a variety of stakeholders.

Stakeholders and Their Roles in Tactical Planning

For any long-term program to be successful, and strategic and tactical plans to be supported, it is crucial that a large number of stakeholder groups are represented in the planning processes. A stakeholder is anyone who has a stake in the success of an organization, school, or school district. School stakeholders are teachers, students, parents, board of education members, central office administrators and supervisors, community representatives, the superintendent of schools, and any other individuals or groups who have a stake in the school or school district. Without a buy-in and a feeling of ownership from a critical mass of stakeholders, strategic and tactical plans will be owned only by the educators and will stand a very narrow chance of successfully being implemented.

It is imperative, however, that these stakeholders learn to function as teams working together to facilitate the planning process.

The levels of common agreement required by stakeholder participation usually require the use of deliberate consensus strategies.

Consensus-Building Techniques

To arrive at agreement among the various stakeholders' interest, it is often necessary to effect specific consensus-building techniques. With the purpose of achieving agreement on strategic and tactical plans, the planning leaders have a choice of numerous consensus-building techniques. The five most frequently utilized include: (1) Polling, (2) Nominal Group Technique, (3) Delphi Technique, (4) Fishbowl Technique, and (5) Telstar (Hoyle, English, & Steffy, 1990; Kaufman & Herman, 1991b).

1. *Polling* is a structured process that involves representative individuals to indicate their preferences or predictions. This can be done by telephone interviews, face-to-face interviews, or by a mail opinionnaire. The results of the polling provide information that assists the strategic planner in devising strategies.
2. *The Nominal Group Technique* is a structured process devised to stimulate new ideas and arrive at consensus. It encourages all to participate, it spotlights discussions on specific questions, and it eventually reaches consensus by a series of voting exercises.
3. *The Delphi Technique* is a structured process for achieving consensus without the requirement of face-to-face contact by the participants. Although designed originally to solicit opinions about the future from experts, it also can be used as a decision-making technique for strategic and tactical planning stakeholders' groups. It could obviously be used to collect the opinions from a broad representation of the community, and this information could then be used by the strategic and/or tactical planning committees' membership. As designed, without modification, the process would follow this sequence:

   • Each participant is asked to write her or his beliefs about the subject specified and send these to the person designated by the school district to coordinate the process.

- These beliefs are then reproduced and distributed to all members selected to participate in the Delphi.

- Each participant is then asked to indicate the items with which she or he both agrees and disagrees. These responses are then returned to the person responsible for conducting the Delphi.

- The results are then listed in two columns (one for agreed-upon items and one for disagreed-upon items); for each item, the number of persons responding in each column is indicated.

- These listings are then forwarded to each participant, with the request that those items to which they disagree be restated in such a manner that the respondent would then agree with the belief.

- This procedure is repeated as many times as needed until final consensus is reached on all items.

4. *The Fishbowl Technique* is one in which a group of representative spokespersons is selected from broader groups to discuss and negotiate points that will lead to consensus while the larger membership observes the dialogue. However, to provide the possibility of input from the observers, provisions are made to allow a rapid input opportunity to anyone who is not a part of the representative discussion group. To illustrate this, a group of eight individuals who represent eight large membership groups is arranged in a close circle of chairs, but an empty chair is also included in the circle for use by audience members who might wish to quickly give input to the discussion. Once the piece of information is given by this temporary audience participant, she or he must return to the audience while the eight representatives continue their dialogue for the purpose of achieving consensus.

5. *Telstar* is another consensus-building technique that is similar to the Fishbowl, but it allows for even broader participation. Telstar can be best used when very large, diverse stakeholders' groups have an interest in the planning results. An example of this technique, beginning with total stakeholder involvement, will clarify its potential use.

- The initial goal of Telstar is to divide large groups into subgroups. If the process is designed to achieve interest and input from a total school district's clientele, the facilitators might go through the initial process with attendees from each school building participating.

- Once the initial exercise is completed, those in attendance are asked to nominate six persons to serve as spokespersons for the local school's interest when meeting with the total school district's group.

- Assuming that there are eight school buildings in the school district, 48 persons (six from each of the eight school buildings) would be asked to come together to attempt to achieve consensus on the issues to be discussed.

- Each of these six-member teams would next be asked to select its primary spokesperson, and the group of eight spokespersons would be seated in chairs in a closely aligned circle. The five other members would be then organized in close formation behind their selected spokesperson.

- Discussion would begin among each of the eight spokespersons; the other five team members would be seated directly behind the primary spokesperson, and the large audience would observe the discussion. The audience could contact the six spokespersons between meetings, but they could not enter the discussions during the official meetings of the eight selected groups.

- However, any of the five members from any group could call for a caucus of her or his group by calling "time out." At this juncture, all eight groups would caucus until the individual who originated the caucus called "time in." During these caucuses, the five members from each group could give their spokesperson ideas or directions. However, once the caucuses are completed, only the eight spokespersons can continue to discuss consensus possibilities.

- This process continues until final consensus is achieved.

A simple diagram will demonstrate the alignment of two of the six-member spokespersons groups.

Not only is it wise to have training of participants in the various techniques for achieving consensus, it is also important that the tactical planning stakeholders be provided with other training activities to ensure the success of their tasks.

Required Staff Development and Training Activities

If a broadly representative group of stakeholders (parents, students, teachers, community representatives, classified employees, and administrators) is organized into a strategic and/or tactical planning committee, it is crucial that, prior to and during their work, the committee members are provided with staff development and training activities that will enhance their effectiveness (Mercer, 1991). This is necessary because committee members will vary from very sophisticated individuals, who have experienced much group work and data gathering and analysis, to those individuals who have never worked in groups before and have never had to collect and analyze important data. Therefore, it is wise for those who are in charge of the planning process to provide training opportunities in the following categories:

- Team building
- Communications skills, such as active listening, wait time, paraphrasing, negotiating meanings, and nonverbal communications

- Consensus-building techniques, such as Polling Nominal Group, Delphi, Fishbowl, and Telstar
- Data gathering, arraying, and analyzing techniques

Roles of Stakeholders

Before ending this chapter it is important to elaborate upon the roles of the various stakeholders in the planning activities, for the ultimate success of the planning efforts will depend upon how well those roles are played.

- The *board of education*, as a whole, and the individual board members should play the roles of officially approving the planning process, officially appointing the committee members, officially receiving and approving the committees' strategic and tactical plans, serving as communication links to the community at large, and acting as cheerleaders for the process and for the stakeholders involved in the planning process. Occasionally, it may be wise to have a single member of the board serve on the planning committees, as this will serve to facilitate an immediate communications link to and from the board and the planning committees.
- The *superintendent of schools*, in all probability, should not serve as an official member of the committees. The superintendent's roles will parallel those of the board members, with the addition of providing for day-to-day resources and data.
- *Central office administrators* can provide data and suggestions in their areas of expertise. They also can serve as cheerleaders for the process and for the stakeholders who form the planning committees. In addition, they can serve as communications links and salespersons to the building-level employees, students, and the broader community. In all probability, to keep the committee from being centrally dominated, it would be wise to have only two of this group serve as official members of the committees, with the others being on call to the committees (Herman, 1989c).

- *Building principals and their assistants* should serve similar roles to those of the central office administrators (Herman, 1989e). Their knowledge of what is happening at the building level is very important information to share, and they have the most direct communications avenues to students, teachers and other building-level employees, parents, and the community which exists within the school's attendance boundaries. Obviously, their support and cheerleading activities are most crucial. Again, to keep the committee from being dominated by administrators, it is wise to have only one elementary principal, one middle or junior high principal, and one senior high principal officially serve on the committees, with the others being on call when requested by the committees.

- *Teachers and other employees* are important stakeholders because they are the ones closest to the students. Without them, education would not take place. This group should have broad representation on the committees, and it would be important to have one representative from each school building in the district. Besides sharing their expertise and being valuable communications links, they can provide detailed data and suggestions to the planning committees.

- *Students* will represent important assets to the committees because they can define the "what is" state of affairs and help define the "what should be" preferred future vision from their view.

- *Parents and community members* are crucial to this process and should be broadly represented on the planning committees. First of all, they are the ones providing the students and paying the taxes. They can assist in collecting soft data (opinions), and the community representatives can assist in collecting hard (factual) data and in projecting trends into the future. This group will also provide the most believable group of communicators to the community at large, and they will have to agree on the preferred future vision to allow the planning to take place that is designed to achieve that preferred future vision.

Now that we have: (1) defined tactical planning, (2) provided a tactical planning model, (3) provided an example of how the model could work in a local school district, (4) discussed helpful consensus-building techniques, (5) provided suggested training experiences designed to make the diverse members of the planning committees more efficient and effective, and (6) clarified the roles of the various stakeholders' groups, we will provide a Tactical Planning Checklist as a means of reviewing the important points covered in Chapter 3.

Tactical Planning Checklist

Directions: Place an X in each box as you complete the steps indicated.

- ☐ The school district's Tactical Planning Committee has been organized and it has broad representation from all stakeholders' groups.
- ☐ The Tactical Planning Committee members clearly understand the definition of tactical planning.
- ☐ The roles of each group's representatives to the Tactical Planning Committee were clear to all members.
- ☐ Training and staff-development activities were consistently woven into the working of the Tactical Planning Committee.
- ☐ As the committee members were attempting to make decisions, consensus-building techniques were taught and utilized.
- ☐ The Tactical Planning Committee reviewed all of the information transmitted from the Strategic Planning Committee for the school district.
- ☐ The Tactical Planning Committee developed numerous specific measurable objectives for each strategic goal submitted to it by the Strategic Planning Committee for the school district.
- ☐ After arriving at all of the strategic objectives, the committee members decided upon a set of decision rules that

allowed them to establish priorities for action among all the goals and objectives.

☐ Once the priorities were established, the committee members developed specific action plans and reached consensus on which alternative suggested action plans would be implemented to achieve each priority objective.

☐ Once the committee members detailed their preferred action plans, they provided detailed answers to the following questions:

- Why is this important?
- What tasks must be performed to bring this action plan to fruition?
- Who was responsible for completing each task within the time lines established?
- When shall each task be completed and the final objective achieved?
- What resources are to be allocated to each action plan?
- How are we going to measure whether the objective has been achieved to a satisfactory qualitative level and within budget and time limits?

☐ A continuous and comprehensive monitoring structure was introduced to tell if each action plan was working well, required modifications, or should be canceled.

☐ Finally, all plans and all results were communicated to the school district's Strategic Planning Committee, because planning can only be successful if both the strategic and tactical plans work in tandem.

Reminders

1. Tactical planners should use decision rules when prioritizing objectives.
2. Use the activities of brainstorming, force field analysis, cost/benefit analysis, and best alternative selection when designing action plans.

3. Monitor each of the action plans.
4. Use consensus-building techniques to facilitate stakeholder involvement and agreement.
5. Provide planning committees with staff development and training.

Summary

Chapter 3 provided information about tactical planning and its uses by administrators. Tactical planning, defined as the methods intended to achieve the strategic plans, requires the development of specific objectives and the application of decision rules about the achievability, affordability, meaningfulness, and chance of success of proposed objectives. The action plans techniques of brainstorming, force field analysis, cost/benefit analysis, and selection of best alternative were described.

Information about a variety of consensus-building techniques, including Polling, Nominal Group, Delphi, Fishbowl, and Telstar, was provided. The chapter also emphasized the requirement for staff development and training activities for those stakeholders and individuals who will become involved in tactical planning activities. The chapter elaborated on the roles that can be played during tactical planning by boards of education, superintendents, central office administrators, building principals and their assistants, teachers, classified employees, students, parents, and community members. A tactical planning checklist was provided.

Basic Tools

ADMINISTRATIVE FRAMEWORKS
FOR PLANNING

A wide variety of tools is useful to administrators as they plan to solve problems, attempt new programs, and improve their schools or school districts. These include: (1) Organizational Development (OD), (2) Management Information Systems (MIS), (3) needs assessments, and (4) Human Resource Development (HRD) activities. OD and HRD are important in that, as structural and functional components for a school, they form the reference framework for planning. The ongoing informational and input activities provided by effective MIS and needs assessment systems are needed to continually inform the planning process. These planning tools are synergistic and reflect the ongoing functions of school districts. Methods of developing a curriculum-linked budget and means of helping teachers, administrators, and other employees with their professional development are included in this chapter as examples of planning activities that draw their impetus and substance directly from the planning process.

Organizational Development (OD)

Organizational Development involves the maintenance and improvement of the total school district and all of its components (individual schools and departments) by: (1) monitoring the current "health" of the organization, (2) scanning the external and internal environments to determine trends and project these trends into the future, (3) determining the future vision of the organization that is desired, (4) identifying the needs (gaps between "what is" and "what should be" or "what could be"), and (5) developing intervention strategies that will assist the educational leaders in achieving the "what should be" or "what could be" future organizational state desired. More important, OD involves continuous planning designed to enhance the entire system's ability for data collection, self-study, and improvement of the entire educational organization or school district. This description relates to the concept of diagnosis, action, and maintenance, which are the basic components of OD. All important decision makers have a role in OD planning activities. The decision makers certainly include the policy-making board of education; the superintendent of schools; the building principals; and the central office administrators, supervisors, employee representatives, consultants, and all categories or organizations of employees.

Regardless of the persons or groups involved in OD responsibilities, there are certain activities that must be addressed when planning strategies to improve an unhealthy organization or when planning to maintain a healthy organization. These activities may vary, depending on the stage of development of the school district (youthful though mature), depending upon the external and internal variables that impact the organization and/or its subparts, and depending upon the stage of development and attitudes of individual employees and groups of employees.

OD is a macro approach, designed to change the entire educational organization in the directions desired to better accommodate a visioned organizational future state. A macro design involves "the overall structure and outline, sequence of parts, and general forms through which activities flow." Obviously, this cannot be achieved without attention to the identified needs (discussed in more detail later in the chapter) of the employees within the school district. Attention to employee needs may be considered attending to micro development needs; the micro design of OD involves particular structural elements, such as groups or individual buildings. Attending to the total organization's needs may be considered attending to the macro development needs. Macro and micro needs are interrelated and overlapping. Both are needed to achieve the highest levels of organizational performance and employee satisfaction. A high-performing organization has a "deep commitment to employees' personal well-being and growth."

As employees change, the organization must plan to attend to these changes and to modify its structures and processes to accommodate the changes. On the other hand, as the total education organization or school district changes because of legislation, community attitudes, union master contracts, technological advancements, or a myriad of other impacting variables, the employees may have to change in order to operationalize the process. Since school systems are traditionally bureaucratic and reluctant to change, having a planning process in place that is a vehicle for change works to overcome the usual entrenched resistance. Organizations must be helped to perceive the need for change at early stages of organizational transformation, rather than delaying until the impacting external variables make it imperative (Herman & Herman, 1991).

Management Information Systems (MIS)

A *Management Information System* should be developed to provide information and feedback opportunity to all levels of employees and to the school district's clients. The MIS should concentrate on those items considered crucial to achievement of the mission of the school district, school building, or other suborganizations of the educational organization. The types of data that can be accrued in such a system reflect the various organizational functions of the school district:

- Information pertaining to the instructional core could include both hard data regarding student grades and achievement or minimum mastery test scores, rates of graduation and retention, dropout rates, and postgraduate employment rates and and soft data derived from questionnaires probing for student and teacher perceptions of the quality of instruction, specific course content, and the outcomes of programs.

- Information pertaining to the array of student services, such as registration, attendance, and personal data information, guidance and counseling, master scheduling, health care, and referrals to other community organizations and agencies, is critical in determining the cost factors (hard data) and client perceptions (soft data) of these provisions.

- The common fixed assets or capital outlay assets inventories (normally carrying lists of furniture and heavier equipment) can be included, on a per-building basis, and can be expanded to include the array of instructional materials (such as secondary science laboratory equipment or primary math kits), textbooks and library volumes, media equipment, and software.

- Operations at the central office level, such as the details of personnel records, and the comprehensive bank of information regarding district finances—budgetary development and internal and external accounting, as well as overall fiscal management—will represent a significant part of any district's MIS.

- Programmatic information, particularly regarding federal and state-mandated programs, such as special education and Chapter I, must be maintained, in terms of both delivery and fiscal management.

- Operational support areas, such as transportation, food service, and maintenance, generate data that should be included. As these areas represent widely dispersed and sometimes greatly varying levels and types of services, on a school-by-school basis, the inclusion of the details and cost of that delivery are critical for district planning, particularly in times of budgetary reduction, since these are areas traditionally cut back first.

The MIS data combinations possible across these categories have the capacity to display in greater detail, for example, large and small cost centers, types and amounts of different equipment, the range of personnel certifications and years/types of experience, and the instructional and personal effects of varying programs on varying subpopulations of students. The district or school planning and decision-making process has a strong advantage in having the ability to view both broad-brush and pinpoint details of the operation on demand (Kaufman & Herman, 1991b). Very comprehensive school MIS software programs are currently on the market that address these data input and processing capacities and offer an array of education-tailored applications. Most school districts already have some level of computer application, at least in the financial management area. The purchase and implementation of a larger and all-encompassing system, however, is costly and causes major change within the schools. Some smaller districts have co-opted to share these services; others have purchased these services from state intermediate agencies or private contractors. Some state departments of education provide fiscal and student data database services to the districts or agencies. There are smaller software programs available that can be used by individual schools for their site-based decision making and planning; these might be desirable options for individual schools to adopt in order to accomplish more accurate and effective planning. (This topic is mentioned again in Chapter 7.)

Needs Assessments

As described in Chapter 2, a need is the discrepancy between current results and the required results. The means of closing the identified gaps are the staff development programs that are created in response to these needs—the gaps between "what is" and "what should be." Needs may reflect larger factors that must be addressed through the strategic planning decision-making process, or they may, in a more focused way, reveal staff development requirements, discussed later in the chapter.

The task of "what is" has been done primarily by scanning the internal and external environments for impacting trends. The "what should be" is completed when the planners reach consensus on the preferred future vision. Identification of needs is an important pre-step to developing the strategic goals for what should be at some future point in time.

As an integral part of strategic planning (see Chapter 2), needs assessments provide an empirical database for planning: They add actual performance data and consequences to the values, beliefs, visions, and missions of strategic planning. It is critical to elicit an accurate and focused response to employees' or clients' perceptions of needs, rather than their description or prescription for an answer to a particular solution or problem (Herman & Herman, 1991). An example would be that of asking, "What writing performance results do we expect of our fifth graders?" rather than "What writing workshop training do we need?" If the needs assessments focus on the three levels of needs described in Chapter 2 (mega, macro, and micro) and ask questions designed to elicit answers expressed in terms of expected and actual outcomes or products (quality of graduates' skills, levels of demonstrated literacy, and so on), then the information obtained will be more useful and will more truly reflect the actual situation of the school or district.

Categories of Useful Hard and Soft Data

Some of the data that are gathered in needs assessments and are input into an MIS to be monitored and evaluated are of the soft data (attitudinal or non-independently verifiable) type, and some are of the hard data (verifiable) type (Kaufman & Herman, 1991b). Some examples of the types of data that may be systematically collected as part of an MIS follow. These data may be computerized, and trends over various time periods can be discerned.

Hard data that could indicate the degree of employee satisfaction with the work environment include: (1) the number of employee absences and tardiness, (2) the number of grievances filed by employees, (3) staff turnover, (4) the reasons for leaving employment with the district that are given at exit interviews with the personnel department's staff, and (5) the number of employees and the number of hours they volunteer for community service or other service. Further examples of categories of hard data could include student ethnic background, primary language, promotions to the next grade or to another school, or honors and awards.

A soft data example is that of a survey provided to a stratified random sampling of each employee group on an established basis. The type of questions included on the survey instrument could deal with such matters as: (1) Do you feel that the board of education, administrators, and other employees care about you? (2) Do you feel you have interesting and important work to perform? (3) Do you feel you are given recognition for your contributions to the building in which you work and to the school district? (4) Do you feel your opinion is sought and listened to as it relates to your work conditions? (5) Do you receive help if and when you have to have it? (6) To what degree are you satisfied with your working conditions (very, some, not at all)? and (7) Given a choice, would you choose to continue working in this school district, or would you prefer working somewhere else? Further soft data examples could include surveys of perceptions of graduates with regard to career preparation and the quality of their current occupations, perceptions of the community regarding the quality of the educational program, and perceptions of a particular population, such as a non-English-speaking minority group, about the multicultural instruction offered by the district.

Human Resource Development (HRD)

Human Resource Development involves all activities within the educational organization or school district that have the potential to either positively or negatively affect the people who work within the school district. Those individuals charged with the responsibility for employee-related activities have as their mission to attend to the activities related to employees in such a manner that the productivity and satisfaction of employees are maximized. This responsibility involves substantial planning—anticipating and avoiding or minimizing the impact of those activities that may negatively impact employees—and it also involves developing activities and making decisions that optimize the satisfaction and productivity levels of employees.

In most educational organizations, especially relatively small school districts, there is not a centralized administrator responsible for coordinating all the human resource activities. Even in large school districts that have a person or a staff responsible for HRD, many persons are involved in implementing and monitoring HRD activities. Some of the major players include principals, staff developers, personnel specialists, superintendents, instructional specialists, trainers, and board of education members (policymakers). The enrollment size of a school district and the proportionate number of professional and classified personnel must define the need for the establishment of a differentiated HRD staff. Inefficiency in planning for the HRD function, when one considers that salaries and benefits alone generally constitute 80% of all school district expenditure, is too costly in terms of service and efficiency. The added HRD functions of staff development and training, discussed further on, expand the need for a coordinated and supported HRD structure. The planning activities of HRD involve the recruitment and induction of personnel, and the planned structures that support their tenure of employment: supervising, appraising, and training.

Planning for recruitment as a process has the major thrust of acquiring the number and type of people necessary for the current and future needs of the district, with the continuous perspective of targeting potential applicants for anticipated vacancies. Certification is a continuing concern in this area, along with affirmative action requirements. Some school districts have paid premium salaries for science and math teachers because they are in short supply. School principals, especially those at the secondary level, sometimes seek out individuals with multiple certifications or endorsements in order to meet changing master schedule and class section needs. Previously, special education teachers were paid additional sums because they were in short supply. Most school districts pay teachers with advanced degrees more than they pay new hires who usually have only bachelor's degrees. These are salary contingencies that must be anticipated in the planning process.

Whenever the district has a vacancy or creates a new position, the persons doing the recruiting and hiring should do two things. First, they should analyze the skills, experience, and other information about all current employees—the development of a profile indicating the status of current human resources. (This type of information concerning all district employees should already exist in a manageable and accessible MIS.) A human resource profile for each job classification should be developed from information gathered from employees. This analysis will identify not only what current employees have to offer but also any areas of weakness or certification gaps that should be filled because of a void within the current employee group, on a long-term basis. Many schools already do this informally as they look for candidates who have skills that fill in or complement existing skills in departments or grade levels.

Immediately upon the new employee's starting her or his work, until the time that the employee retires from the school district's service or terminates employment with the district for any cause, that employee is in the development phase of HRD. Planning should be done to ensure clarity of terms in the selection and contracting process, and subsequent planning should be taken to assign the new employee to maximize both district benefit and employee success. Planned assistance for the new employee should be supported with peer contacts and supervisor-provided transitional activities that will facilitate the induction experience.

Planning for the formal supervisory and appraisal process, however legally and compliance-driven, should be done to maximize the function for both employer and employee. Employee involvement in the development of supervisory and appraisal procedures is vital for morale and for due process purposes. Both the formative and summative evaluation processes should be documented and aimed at professional growth. Training and staff development are logical operational components of such an appraisal system (Herman & Herman, 1991).

The four tools—OD, MIS, needs assessments, and HRD— should be considered as integrated and continuous parts of overall school planning. As such, they are operational in nature and support the tactical planning process. Examples of how they can be applied to everyday school functions are provided in the following descriptions.

Developing a Curriculum-Linked Budget

A curriculum-linked budget demands allocation of a school's discretionary funds based on the needs assessments and data collection processes described earlier in this chapter and in Chapter 2. It will reflect the strategic planning process in that it is a communal, assessment-based, priority-setting approach. Planning for such budgeting will establish that:

- Budgetary requests should be built in incremental, programmatic form.
- There must be active principal and teacher participation.
- The cost/benefit of each program, such as a reduction in the average class size, must be delineated.
- Priorities must be rank-ordered by a school decision-making body, such as that described in Chapter 7.
- It must be formatted in a presentable way so that budgetary allocations, fixed costs, salary commitments, and current levels and areas of expenditure are clearly discernible. (Poston, 1992)

Consideration and deliberation regarding the technical core of curriculum and instruction (as part of the overall organizational development) are done during the internal scanning and goal and objective setting process of strategic planning. As each school determines the operational planning thrust of that larger process, the selected curricular goals and objectives should be designed into budgetary packages and ranked according to the decision makers' priorities (Zenger & Zenger, 1992). These priorities should likewise be determined by consideration of curricular and instructional needs assessments and by ongoing input from the MIS. An example of this is provided at the end of the chapter.

Helping Teachers, Administrators, and Classified Employees Develop Professionally

There are three important dimensions of needs assessment within a school district that require staff development programs; they relate to the total school district, subgroups within the school district, and individual employees of the school district. As part of the overall process of the district's development of Human Resources, these dimensions provide a conceptual framework for planning the delivery of staff development services.

The needs that affect everyone in the total school district, and for which staff development activities are appropriate interventions, might well come from external or demographic changes. For example, the change of a school district's student composition from one of practically all white students to one comprised mostly of a mix of African-American, Asian, and Mexican-American students should create the need for staff development activities for all employees, relating to the differing cultures and the communication skills required to successfully deal with a new student-body mix.

As a technological and new training example, once the school district is committed to getting all of its professional personnel computer literate, it requires staff development activities related to computer use and operation by every teacher, teacher aide, and administrator in the total school district. Both examples of needs would have been revealed by the process of strategic planning and by targeted surveys of training needs.

Subgroup needs can come from a wide variety of sources, and each identified need can be met by a staff development activity geared to that specific identified need. Examples include (1) the training of all elementary teachers in the whole language approach to language arts; (2) the training of all industrial teachers in the use of robotics, once the school district has included robotics in its machine-related industrial courses; (3) the training of all elementary teachers in the whole language approach to language arts; and (4) the training of all teachers in the technique of cooperative learning.

Individual needs can best be identified on an ongoing basis by using staff evaluation as the method of needs assessment. Evaluation, in this case, is formative in nature and is a cooperative activity between the individual employee and the supervisor. In the case of a teacher, it could be training aimed at the improvement of classroom management. In the case of an administrator, it could be training intended to sharpen observational and supervisory skills. Once the needs are identified, an individualized staff development program can be devised, with some offerings being provided in a menu format. For planning purposes, both individual and subgroup needs can be considered micro needs, in the sense of being intended for a smaller group, rather than for system-wide needs.

There is an overlap and feedback area in needs identified during evaluation and those addressed during the development activities. Once the staff development activities have assisted the individual in meeting the identified needs, the individual can move on to other needs that have been identified, and staff development activities can be provided that will assist the individual in becoming even more productive. This is a process that can best be planned and monitored through the use of the MIS; any and all determined needs of the district, at whatever delivery level, should be included as part of that system.

Before any program of staff development or, for that matter, of staff evaluation can take place, there are four planning prerequisite conditions that must be present if the program is to be successful: (1) felt need (as determined by needs assessments), (2) human resources, (3) financial resources, and (4) temporal resources.

A *felt need* must exist before any program can be successfully begun. If the individual teacher does not feel a need to use a computer with her or his students, that teacher will probably not be interested in spending time and effort in staff development activities related to computer knowledge and usage. On the other hand, an employee in the business office who uses the computer to do the day-to-day work will readily participate in training sessions to learn the new upgraded software applications, because that knowledge is an absolute necessity for job performance. A curriculum director may see no need to participate in a staff development program directed at improving administrators' skills in conducting formative evaluation conferences with teachers. On the other hand, a principal who concurred with his supervisor that one area of operation where much improvement could be made was that of conducting formative teacher evaluation conferences would readily volunteer to participate in a staff development program geared to this clearly identified need.

Once the felt need has been established, the other prerequisite planning conditions of human resources, financial resources, and temporal resources have to be met if the staff development program is to be successful. The *human resources* required might include a critical mass of employees to make the staff development cost-effective; it might include the release of some of the district's employees who have specific skills to act as trainers; or it might include the hiring of consultants to perform the specific training. *Financial resources* will probably include money to hire substitutes for the employees during the staff development training periods, money for consultants and for the necessary equipment, and supplies and housing for the participants. *Temporal resources* not only include the released time for the district's employees who are taking the training or who are serving as trainers but should also include time for administrators to be present to provide visible and active support for the employees who are involved in the staff development activities. In fact, some of the most successful staff development activities will be those where administrators and teachers attend the activities as teams.

Once the prerequisite conditions have been met, six questions should be addressed before proceeding with the staff development plans. The questions of why, who, how, what, when, and where must be answered when one is planning a staff development system.

- *Why* should a school district operate a staff development program? The why of staff development should be to provide training that will help the individual employee improve the areas identified as needs through the formative evaluation process.
- *Who* should be involved in staff development activities should include in-district trainers, supervisors, out-of-district consul-

tants, and those who are participating in the training activities.

- The *What* question depends on the specific staff development activities that are designed to address the specific needs identified.

- The *Where* of staff development activities will vary from the workplace to off-site locations, depending on the specific needs being addressed and the specific environment desired. The location for the training should reflect training requirements rather than preferences. Use of school facilities—an individual campus site itself—has been recommended in order to facilitate trainee awareness of application and participation.

- The *When* for staff development may take place during the workday by hiring substitutes to release employees during the training period, but many times this is not desirable because students should not be deprived of their regular teacher too frequently or for long time periods. Many other employees also cannot be separated from their normal duties frequently or for long periods of time. In these cases, it is many times more reasonable to offer staff development activities during after-school hours, weekends, or normal vacation periods. There is evidence, however, to support a choice of time that will maximize the participants' motivation. The delivery of staff development at a noncontractual time, and under the assumption of participants' willingness to volunteer the hours, has almost a guarantee of failure. Some compensation for the volunteered time, whether monetary, in the form of staff development credit hours, or through other compensatory measures, should be provided.

- The *How* of staff development will vary with the specific needs being addressed. For example, if the training activity is to train teachers to develop or use videocassettes in their teaching, the activities would be specifically geared to developing and utilizing video equipment during the training. If, however, the training is designed to improve the administrators' ability to carry out formative evaluation conferences, the how might well combine analysis of videos showing examples of administrators conducting formative conferences with practice activities conducted during the training sessions. Effective staff development programs, in general, include such characteristics as participant involvement and positive attitudes, planning for training transfer and continuation support and mechanisms, an andragogical activities orientation, a tangible-results focus, and the provision for specificity and concreteness of instruction (Herman & Herman, 1991).

Examples

Curriculum-Linked Budget

Corwin Elementary School, through its strategic and tactical planning process and in concert with the larger strategic and tactical planning process at the district level, has determined that it will target specific gains in mathematics test scores and student demonstrations of proficiency this year. Both hard and soft data emerging from needs assessment support this choice. The budgetary process reflects this focus, in that the principal and staff:

- Create proposed budgetary packages around appropriate supportive instructional materials, both in software and in other media materials
- Plan for math tutorial support funds to be set aside for underachieving students
- Target the earlier developmental years with budgetary choices of math manipulative kits, selected to complement existing materials and textbook adoptions
- Budget for staff development for at least one teacher per grade level in the *Math Their Way* program

Three Types of Staff Development

Staff Development—An Individual Activity: The school district's graphic artist has never had the opportunity to discover the use of computers for graphic renderings. The graphic artist requested such training, and the HRD Director freed sufficient funds from the budget to allow the graphic artist to attend a one-month's workshop on computer graphics that was held in New York City during the summer. Although this workshop, for which the district paid all related costs, was expensive, the graphic artist is now able to produce an increase of 80% in the amount of high-quality graphics intended for classroom usage.

Staff Development—A Subgroup Activity: Through review of the accident reports by the Director of Transportation and through discussions with bus drivers about their staff development needs, it was clear that additional training was required to avoid a future serious accident, to reduce the number of minor accidents, and to make the bus drivers feel more in control during the stormy winter months. The HRD department arranged to have the police barricade a stretch of highway for one half-day, and the district arranged to have foam placed on that patch of highway to simulate snowy and icy winter conditions. After detailed instruction on how to avoid skids and accidents during poor winter weather conditions, each bus driver was provided numerous opportunities to practice safely controlling a bus during these simulated winter weather conditions.

Staff Development—A Total Employees Example: The school district purchased a computer system for use by the employees of the entire school district. This system was to be used by all clerical personnel; by the dispatcher in the bus garage; by all personnel in the business, instructional, and personnel offices; by all building-level administrators; by the warehouse supervisor; and by teachers and students for instructional purposes. This decision was made to keep the district abreast of computer technology. The task of the staff development specialist became one of training all employees in the use of this new computerized technology. A series of training activities was established, differentiated by category of employee and type of computer applications to be used in performing specific jobs. In some cases, consultants were hired to handle highly technical training; in some cases teachers who had used the new computer system previously were hired to offer workshops on weekends and after normal school hours for other teachers; and in other cases on-line technical assistance was provided on an as-needed basis for personnel in the business office (Herman & Herman, 1991).

Reminders

1. In planning for OD, stress the macro approach and the attention given to micro needs. OD involves the maintenance and improvement of the total school district and all its components and is dynamically interactive with HRD.

2. In considering HRD planning, anticipate substantial planning aimed at the development of activities and the making of employee decisions that optimize the satisfaction and productivity levels of employees.

3. Plans for needs assessments should provide the critical perceptual temperature of individuals within a system and can supplement the hard and soft data that are critical to school planning. These and other data are most readily accessible through a comprehensive MIS system.

4. Ensure that the larger, long-term goals and objectives addressing the technical core of curriculum and instruction are reflected in annual budgetary expenditure.

5. Keep a constant awareness that the purpose of staff development is performance improvement, and that a school's or district's planned HRD activities achieve that purpose through an andragogically designed staff development and training system.

Summary

The chapter discussed a wide variety of tools that are useful to administrators as they plan to solve problems, attempt new programs, and improve their schools or school districts. The major tools of systemic structure and function, OD and HRD, were presented as planning frameworks aimed at the system's ability for data collection, self-study, and the improvement of the entire school or school district. HRD was presented as involving all activities within the educational organization or school district that have the potential of positively or negatively affecting the people who work within the school district. Such specifics as planned personnel recruitment and induction were discussed.

Needs assessments were described as an integral part of strategic planning, providing an empirical database for planning. Such a database is part of a recommended MIS, which serves as a storage place for information from the various organizational functions of the school district, including both hard (verifiable) data and soft data (attitudinal or non-independently verifiable).

The linkage between a curricular-driven budget and the previously established curricular goals and objectives of a school was established. The chapter ended with a consideration of the planning and resources needed for staff development for teachers and other staff members and a focus on the three types of needs—total group, subgroup, and individual—which can be met by planned and focused staff development.

Workable Techniques

FACILITATING THE PLANNING PROCESS

C hapter 5 concentrates on discussions about specific techniques that are useful for administrators involved in various types of planning. Techniques discussed include: (1) Program Evaluation Review Technique (PERT), (2) a modified PERT technique, (3) Critical Path Method (CPM), (4) Management by Objectives (MBO), (5) focus groups, (6) action plans, (7) issue papers, (8) narrow and wide lens tactical planning, (9) simulations, and (10) marketing and selling techniques. These techniques are intended to facilitate the planning process through the logical analysis of the existing school district environment, the effective determination and communication of a district's planning thrust and direction, and the efficient making of district decisions.

Program Evaluation Review Technique (PERT)

This is a network-based tool for planning, such as planning the implementation of an educational system. This technique programs each detailed task and activity along an identified time line, thus providing a blueprint for displaying events to be accomplished and the person(s) responsible for carrying out the activity within the time frame indicated (Miller, 1974). The plan is a complex visual schematic that allows for tracking and a comprehensive all-in-one-glance at the progress of the planned project or task. The flexibility of a PERT chart allows for the expression of anticipated minimum and maximum execution times for each of the activities and events (Herman & Kaufman, 1991). It is particularly valuable when a planned project is so innovative that there are no task or time experiential comparisons to be made. An example might be that of the installation of on-line automated attendance capacities at each school, where the individual configuration of each site's prewiring (or lack of it) for such technology would preclude reasonable task and time estimation. A modified PERT, reflecting a simpler methodology, may also be used; an example is provided at the end of the chapter.

Critical Path Method (CPM)

This is another type of critical path analysis planning, very similar to PERT. CPM, however, is used when a planned project, such as the construction of an elementary school with a standard type of district K-5 architecture, has very well-known subtasks and where, due to the multiple construction history of elementary schools, for example, the time estimates are reasonably well known. Whereas PERT is more event-oriented and nonexperience-based, CPM is activity-oriented and experience-based (Banghart & Trull, 1973).

Management by Objectives (MBO)

MBO is a strategy of planning to attain improved results in managerial actions, seeking to maximize organizational efficiency while meeting the needs of participants. It is characterized by:

- A focus on what is expected in terms of objectives and performance criteria
- A direct linkage to the budget process
- The fostering of teamwork through the identification of common goals

- The programming of work by the setting of terminal dates for accomplishment of specific tasks
- The facilitation of compensation, providing a rational basis for rewarding performance and accomplishment

MBO is tied to strategic planning in that the specific tactical or operating objectives emerging from the planning are tied to a district's or school's budgetary process; and the MBO objectives determined by each individual carrying out the plan's agreed-upon strategies, mission, and goals serve as the linkage between strategic and operational planning. In general, MBO appears to plan strategically for the future through the involvement of both managers and subordinates in their areas of responsibility (Mercer, 1991).

Focus Groups

The technique of focus groups is a planning/problem-solving technique that involves calling together like-job employee groups or vertical decision teams to discuss specific topics of importance. It can be used as a standard structure to address any problems that arise, or it can be convened on an as-needed basis. These focus groups can be presented with any planning data that has been arrayed, and they can discuss ways of solving, clarifying, or improving planning concerns and decision-making processes. Like-job groups will deal with the decision-making process from the standpoint of decisions being made within their group and will also deal with decisions that their group has in conjunction with other groups within the matrix organization of the school district or educational organization (Herman & Herman, 1991).

Action Plans

These are the tactical operational plans that clearly and comprehensively describe the execution details of a specific set of tasks and procedures designed to achieve one or more of the objectives of the strategic plan (Herman, 1990a). They are a standard feature of the strategic planning process and are used to operationalize the established long-term goals. As an example, once the planners of a school district outline the supporting and restraining factors for each suggested solution, they can go to the challenge of devising the detailed action plan for the alternative of their choice. The simplified version that follows uses a totally different objective from that previously discussed. The approach illustrated follows the following action plan steps: (1) determine all the detailed tasks to be accomplished, without consideration of the chronology for which they will be done, to speed up the planning process; (2) once all tasks are listed, place them in chronological order (for example, when building a house, you don't want the electricians scheduled after the plasterers have enclosed the walls); (3) decide which specific person or persons have the responsibility of completing that task; and (4) predetermine the date at which each task is to be completed (Herman & Herman, 1991).

For our example, let us assume that the objective agreed to by the strategic planners was to devise a recognition program for all of the school district's employees. The district's employees came up with a detailed action plan:

A cost/benefit analysis should also be conducted for each alternative, and one should definitely be conducted after the selected alternative has been made operational. If the cost/benefit analysis is done on all the alternatives being considered, the planners have to predict the ratio of cost to benefit. If, however, it is conducted after the alternative has been put into operation, it can become part of the evaluation structure—both formative evaluation and summative evaluation. This type of analysis is valuable in determining the worth of what you get for what you pay. For example, is an expenditure of an additional $100 per potential student dropout a reasonable expenditure to reduce the dropout rate by 10%? Will the expenditure of $1,000 per potential dropout per year provide equivalent or greater benefit than the expenditure if the dropout rate is lowered by 50%? These are the types of questions that can be related to the computation of a ratio of benefit to cost. After the force field analysis and the cost/benefit have been done for each alternative, the selected solution should be put into operation.

Once the action plan is completed, the operational stage is conducted. During the operation of the action plan, the predetermined *formative evaluation* monitoring structures are utilized. Once the operational action plan has been completed, the predetermined *summative evaluation* structures are used. It is at this point that a decision is made to eliminate the specific operational action plan, continue it as previously planned, or modify it and put the altered action plan into place within the school district. Not only is the operational action plan reviewed, but the results must also be related to the strategic plan to verify that it is in compliance with the vision, mission, goals, and objectives that were established during the strategic planning (Herman, 1989c).

Issue Papers

This planning/problem-solving technique utilizes the wealth of alternate ideas created by brainstorming and can be used within the strategic planning process or as a stand-alone planning or decision-making strategy. It is a culminating type of activity, creating a clarified planning proposal or alternative as an outcome of the preceding processes.

Narrow and Wide Lens Tactical Planning

Chapter 3 defined tactical planning as the *hows* to achieve the *whats* that are developed in the strategic planning process. Narrow and wide lens tactical planning are distinguished by a difference in focus, that is, the targeting of a specific, individual problem or need (such as an action plan addressing the upgrading of a biology lab at a high school), versus the more broad employee recognition plan outlined in the sample action plan (see Table 5.1).

Simulations

These are planning practice exercises that are designed to hone the skills of planners and prepare them for actual situations in

TABLE 5.1 An Employee Recognition Action Plan

Tasks	Chronology in Weeks	Who's Responsible	When to Be Completed
Develop recognition programs	2	Each administrator and building's employees	Oct. 19—
Decide upon recognition awards	3	Each administrator and building's employees	Oct. 19—
Determine the cost of each recognition program and of the total recognition effort	4	Business manager	Nov. 19—
Arrange for production or purchase of the awards	6	Business manager and building administrators	Jan. 19—
Decide upon the times and places for granting the awards	7	Planning committee	Feb. 19—
Determine the interest level of employees in initiating an employee recognition system	1	Planning committee	Sept. 19—
Determine the source of funds to operate the program	5	Business manager and superintendent	Nov. 19—

Develop an evaluation system to determine the effectiveness of the program and conduct the evaluation	9	Planning committee	Annually, in May
Conduct the awards activities	8	Employees, planning committee, and administrators	Annually, in April and May
Other tasks	10+	?	?

strategic and tactical planning. They could be used in a training situation, particularly in the initial strategic and tactical planning process. Such an exercise could very well be budgetary in nature, for example, requiring the planners at a given school to assume a scenario of substantial reduction in state budgetary funds, due to revenue shortfall, and create a school budget that reflects a corresponding decrease but protects the technical core of instruction as much as possible.

Marketing and Selling Techniques

The planning process has many constituencies and publics. A strategic plan should be marketed to the nonparticipating members of the school district, to the community, and to other such organizations as the local chamber of commerce and the state department of education. Information about the plan should be provided to the board, the public, and the media. Marketing could include such enhancements as a professionally published final report; media products (videos, slide presentations, and the like) that chronicle the process; and a formal marketing campaign to sell the mission and vision of the district and each school via posters, buttons, and so on. The internal selling must be on a continual basis, as training is provided to facilitate the plan and as there is a concerted effort to ensure that all levels of the district feel there is activity that will accomplish the plan's mission (Mauriel, 1989; Mercer, 1991). The external selling should also be continual, keeping the public informed about the ongoing progress of the school district with regard to the strategic and tactical planning process.

Example

Modified PERT

Task Completed	Chronology	Person Responsible for Completion	Time	How Measured	When

Reminders

1. Use visual tactical tools to track the progress of planning projects, such as PERT and CPM, to simplify the planning monitoring process.

2. Use MBO to tie tactical or operating objectives to a district's or school's budgetary process and to involve both managers and subordinates in their support of a strategic plan.

3. Employ such combined techniques as action plans and issue papers to achieve one or more of the objectives of the strategic plan.

4. Market strategic and tactical plans to ensure internal and external support.

Summary

The chapter discussed a wide variety of tactics that are useful to administrators as they undertake the planning and decision-making process. The PERT technique programs each detailed task and activity along an identified time line and provides a blueprint for displaying events to be accomplished. Critical path analysis planning is similar to PERT, but is used when a planned project has very well-known subtasks and where the time estimates are reasonably well known. PERT is more event-oriented and nonexperience-based; CPM is activity-oriented and experience-based.

MBO is a strategy of planning to attain improved results in managerial actions, seeking to maximize organizational efficiency while meeting the needs of participants. It operationalizes the strategic plan. The technique of focus groups is a planning/problem-solving technique that involves calling together like-job employee groups or vertical decision teams to discuss specific topics of importance. Fishbone analysis is similar in that it considers the cause-and-effect dimensions of a planning problem.

Action plans are those tactical operational plans that clearly and comprehensively describe the execution details of a specific set of tasks and procedures designed to achieve one or more of the objectives of the strategic plan. During the operation of the action plan, the predetermined formative evaluation monitoring structures are utilized. Once the operational action plan has been completed, the predetermined summative evaluation structures are used.

The issue paper is a planning/problem-solving technique that utilizes the wealth of alternate ideas created by brainstorming, the array of supporting and restraining factors generated by force field analysis, and the detailed action plans.

The chapter concludes with a description of the differences between the more narrow and specific problem-targeting and the broader focus of narrow and wide lens tactical planning; the consideration of simulations as planning exercises; and the need to effectively market the planning process and outcome, both internally and externally.

6

Effective Schools

PLANNING FOR SCHOOL SUCCESS

The implementation of the research outcomes and components of effective schools has been a strong trend within the educational practice for more than a decade. Such implementation has been clearly linked to school improvement and is a consistent feature of school reform and restructuring efforts.

Chapter 6 defines effective schools and discusses tactical plans that will create and maintain such schools. The development of these administrative plans and implementation strategies, as related to the findings of effective schools' research, is intended to provide a school improvement framework for individual school planning. The development of an MIS, previously described in Chapter 4, is needed as the database to inform effective school implementation efforts. Methods of monitoring tactical plans, and evaluating the effectiveness of the tactical plans that were initiated to create effective schools, are presented.

Defining Effective Schools

An effective school is one in which the conditions are such that student achievement data show that all students evidence an acceptable minimum mastery of those essential basic skills that are prerequisite to success at the next level of schooling. The effective schools formula that was popularized by Edmonds in 1979 and other researchers consists of seven factors:

- Sense of mission
- Strong building leadership
- High expectations for all students and staff
- Frequent monitoring of student progress
- A positive, orderly learning climate
- Sufficient opportunity for learning
- Parent/community involvement (Levine, 1991)

Most of the school improvement projects that have characterized the last decade included elements of the body of effective schools research and common practice (Herman & Herman, 1993).

Developing Tactical Plans

The strategic planning process, implemented in a district and subsequently in its schools, will create a structure from which the process for district and school improvement can flow. Planning operationally for such improvement, and framing it around the effective schools research and practice base, demands tactical strategies and activities to support each of the correlates, interwoven with the predetermined goals and objectives of the strategic plan's blueprint. Consideration must be given to the varying dimensions of implementing a strategically driven tactical plan. It will become the operationalization of action plans that support the district's strategic plan in the areas of school climate, management, instruction, and curricular goals and objectives.

Creating an MIS

As in the strategic process, a more targeted and school-specific assessment and systematic collection of hard and soft data, including instructionally current practices and attitudes, must be done to identify the strengths, needs, and resources. To work as a school improvement planning team, teachers and other professionals will need the database created by achievement and other information available. This type of hard data should include:

- Campus size, enrollment, and profiles of staff members
- Students' gender, ethnic, and family structure types
- Stability and turnover indicators: cohorts of students arranged by length of time enrolled at the school
- Student conduct: numbers and percent relating to categories of disciplinary action, from initial actions to suspensions and expulsions
- Attendance by grading periods
- Standardized test data and grades per class or subject per grading period
- Levels of participation in student activities and types of participation, such as student government and athletics
- Parental involvement statistics: PTA membership, volunteer numbers and hours, nature of parental participation in school activities
- Professional growth of staff: topics, hours, and numbers participating
- Staff attendance
- Informal data, such as opinionnaires, parent perceptions, and so on

The main point is that to be meaningful with regard to school improvement and effective schools research, these data must be *disaggregated by gender, by ethnic group, and by the socioeconomic status of students* (Lezotte, 1989). Unless the trends of subpopulations are revealed, the school's planning team cannot identify specific areas of nonperformance or group need. For example, if there is math underachievement among seventh-grade girls, or if there is over-representation of a certain socioeconomic group (usually determined by Chapter I or Free and Reduced Lunch family income eligibility information) in student government, or if one particular age-cohort of students shows a longitudinal tendency for problems in writing skills, such information is important to planners as they consider ways to implement the effective schools correlates. Likewise, the data should be disaggregated into programmatic categories, such as the achievement and attitudinal information about the subpopulations of students participating in such differentiated programs as Chapter I, special education, gifted and talented, or English as a Second Language (ESL). These programmatic data should likewise be disaggregated by gender, ethnic group, and socioeconomic status of students.

There is instrumentation available that probes the perceptual levels of students, teachers, other employees, and parents about both the existence and the levels of quality of each of the effective schools correlates; school climate assessment instruments are indeed abundant. This type of information should be gathered, and disaggregated, as described above. Teacher, other employee, and parent information should be particularly analyzed for any grade level or class/subject area trends.

Initiating and Maintaining the Tactical Plans to Implement the Correlates

There are three stages of the school improvement process: *mobilization, implementation* (as noted in Chapter 4), and *institutionalization* (Cox, French, & Houcks-Horsley, 1987). A marketing approach, described in Chapter 5, should be aimed at creating awareness of the planning process. If possible, all staff and representative stakeholders (parents and community members) should be involved in the tactical planning, which will be the natural outcome of the district-level strategic planning process. The introduction and initiation of such plans should mobilize personnel by establishing the commitment of leadership and by assigning roles and responsibilities as the development of implementation game plans for the school. The time and setting for this will be determined by the school calendar and by the time lines set by the district strategic plan. A retreat setting is ideal since it can enhance a desirable sense of collegiality and provide a distinctive and focused purpose effect.

The array of data, already analyzed for trends (such as those described previously) and discernible directions/patterns by a committee(s) charged with this purpose, should be shared with the entire staff prior to coming together as a planning team, and the hard and soft data district-level scanning outcomes likewise displayed. (The trend analyses may also be done by an entire school if the staff size is manageable and if there is sufficient planning time available.) The strategic goals and objectives of the district, and any action plans that have been designed to meet them, should also be displayed. It is helpful to have individual hard copy sets of the data for each participant to keep for current and future reference, and to have wall posters and/or several overhead projectors displaying the same data. Then, with constant visual reference to the district strategic perspective, and informed by the array of school trends and current/longitudinal data, the school's planners can collectively begin to set their goals and objectives. These should be determined on a school-wide basis and, in a corresponding and supportive manner, by each grade level, department, or program area. The techniques for planning described in Chapter 5 should be employed in the school team planning process. A logical progression might be:

- Brainstorm school needs as indicated by the defined trends and data displays.
- Use consensus techniques (such as the Nominal Group or Delphi) to limit the brainstorming outcomes to a manageable list of goals and objectives.
- Brainstorm and limit by consensus the strategies and activities that will support each goal and objective.
- Get cost estimates of implementing each of the proposed strategies and activities. This may be somewhat streamlined or done ahead of time by having standard costs available, such as an average cost for student tutorials, average teacher daily release time and training costs, and so on. If there are unusual proposals that require individual costing, it may be

done as a step scheduled between planning sessions. It is also possible to omit the cost factor for the interim and create the prioritized list of goals and objectives with the intent of costing later and applying resources at the end of the process to see how far down the list the funds will cover.

- Apply the tactical planning decision rules—achievable, affordable, meaningful, and with an 80% chance of success—described in Chapter 3, to further refine the goals and objectives.

- Apply the force field analysis technique to each goal and objective proposal to further limit the list. This process could be assigned to subgroups of staff members, with consensus techniques again applied to prioritize the proposals after the individual sets of supporting/constraining factors have been shared with the whole group.

- If not done previously, apply the resources—discretionary budget funds, available teacher release time, volunteer hours, and so on—to the final list of goals and objectives, each one's cost being determined by the corresponding strategies and activities.

- Do a collective quality and articulation check, realigning the selected goals and objectives with the district strategic plan, and classify each goal and objective with one or more of the effective schools correlates. Officially approve and adopt, as a school, the final goals and objectives. Appoint a group to plan for internal and external marketing of the plan, such as the dissemination of the goals and objectives through district and school newsletters, slogans on buttons, posters, and other communicative strategies. Appoint another group to develop and determine the types of evaluations that will measure each goal and objective. Each grade level and department should then meet individually to determine the collective classroom activities that will support the strategies of the adopted goals and objectives. Each teacher and staff member should also be responsible for individual objective setting (MBO, as described in Chapter 5) to support the school, grade level, or departmental strategies.

Monitoring the Tactical Plans

Within the school setting, it may be helpful to create monitoring structures or committees framed around the seven effective school correlates. It is desirable that these extend across grade levels or be interdepartmental in membership to sustain a whole-school, collegial view of the implementation of the school improvement process. Each committee can set up structures to monitor the implementation of its correlate-related strategies. These structures may include such activities as information-gathering visits with school individuals or groups on a prescheduled basis, monitoring of grade averages per subject per subpopulation at predetermined intervals, or frequent correlate-related informal assessment instruments of perceived levels and quality of the school improvement implementation. These committees can report on a scheduled basis to the whole school, at staff or other meetings, or through written communiques.

At the principal and central office level, there should be overall facilitation (through consultation with groups, logistical arrangements, purchasing, arranging for training, and so on) and monitoring of the plan. The proposed support of the grade-level/departmental and individual activities and objectives should be incorporated into the staff evaluation process (and checked through classroom use monitoring) and should be included in the overall action plan and time line format shown in the example. It would be desirable for each of the grade levels/departments to have a similar action plan, developed with the assistance of the principal. As the results of standardized tests are returned at different times during the year, an organized dissemination plan should facilitate the distribution of the scores to each grade level/department and to parents/stakeholders. Since they usually reflect all-school data, the entire staff should meet to analyze and compare trends and link them with previous longitudinal test data to determine if any fine-tuning of the predetermined school improvement strategies is warranted.

Evaluating the Tactical Plans

A continual data-gathering process, intended for input into the MIS, should be in place. As the effective school committees gather anecdotal and informal soft data information, as student grades accumulate over the various grading periods, and as hard test data come in, they should be stored for the end of the school year and for the staff's review. Some formal and focused time, perhaps in a retreat setting as before, is needed. It is helpful to use the same display of goals, objectives, and strategies on posters and charts, with the new data likewise arrayed. The predetermined evaluative techniques (such as follow-up informal assessment about the presence and quality of each of the effective school correlates, measures of percentile gains in specific areas of norm-referenced tests, and end-of-year grade level and subject area averages of disaggregated groups) should be applied, and the resulting array of outcomes and accomplishments again realigned and compared with the selected goals and objectives of the district strategic plan. Internal and external marketing and celebration of the outcomes and accomplishments should follow.

Example

One of Corwin Elementary School's selected goals for school improvement was an increase in both the average grades and the standardized test percentile levels of overall language arts skills. This was in alignment with one of the district strategic goals, that of producing competent and job-marketable graduates, and in alignment with a related district strategic objective to develop graduates with exemplary communications skills. The need was clearly established by review of previous grades and test scores and was, as revealed by disaggregation, somewhat concentrated in the subpopulation of students in grades K-3 who spoke a second language at home, and also in the cohort of recently enrolled (within the last year) upper-grade-level boys receiving Chapter I services.

Campus Action Plan

Goal: To increase the school's average numerical grade in overall language arts skills from 79 to 85, and to increase the school's percentile level of the standardized achievement test's language arts battery from 70 to 75.

Objective: To maintain or improve the present level of language arts achievement and to provide instructional intervention for all ESL students and selected Chapter I students.

Effective School Correlate: High expectations for all students and staff.

Strategies	Staff Responsible	Resource	Monitoring Activities	Evaluation
Staff training in ESL strategies workshop	Selected teachers	$500 for substitutes and registration fees	Participants will share workshop learning at meetings; principal will observe follow-up lessons	Increase in test scores and grade average
Tutorial for Chapter I students	Volunteers	New tutorial materials of high interest, low-ability language kits	Classroom and Chapter I teachers will monitor and informally test and rediagnose, if needed	Same

TABLE 6.1 Corwin Elementary School's Sample of Disaggregated Standardized Test Percentile Scores in Primary Grades' Language

Grade	Total School	Asian	African-American	Mexican-American	White	Boys	Girls	Ch I	G/T	ESL
First	70	92	87	57	90	85	92	67	95	58
Second	72	89	78	60	88	80	89	69	97	61
Third	75	91	74	55	85	73	82	62	94	57

Reminders

1. Use the effective correlates' language and knowledge base as a basis for collegial dialogue and an organizing framework for school improvement.
2. Use a collegial, team-driven, consensus-building, and inclusive process in planning.
3. Employ the planning tools and strategies presented in previous chapters.
4. Collect as much meaningful hard and soft data as possible, disaggregated where appropriate.
5. Align the school goals and objectives with the district ones.

Summary

This chapter presented an effective schools/school improvement framework and process for individual school planning. A brief description of the effective schools correlates base of research and practice preceded a description of tactical planning and the recommended inclusion of a myriad of hard and soft data in an MIS. The importance of disaggregating data into demographic and programmatic categories achieving detail of display and facilitating trend analysis was stressed. A list of implementation steps outlined the school improvement planning process and incorporated models, procedures, and strategies from preceding chapters. Structures for monitoring and evaluating the improvement process were framed around the effective schools correlates and included formal and informal checkpoints, review of hard and soft data as it accumulated over the academic year, and the inclusion of the selected improvement strategies in an MBO-enhanced staff evaluation. Samples of a school action plan and test score disaggregation were provided.

School-Based Management

PLANNING FOR SHARED

DECISION MAKING

L ike effective schools and school improvement programs, the implementation of School-Based Management (SBM) and shared decision making has been a distinct trend within educational practice for more than a decade. Similarly, this implementation has been clearly linked to school improvement and is also a consistent feature of school reform and restructuring efforts. As a vehicle for strategic and tactical planning, SBM provides a participatory and decision-making framework for the operationalizing of planning.

Chapter 7 defines SBM and discusses tactical plans that will help initiate and maintain SBM in schools. The SBM implementation process includes (1) deciding on an SBM committee structure, (2) determining the areas and degrees of decision-making authority, (3) developing by-laws and building-level policies, (4) developing training programs for the participants, (5) conducting a needs assessment, (6) deciding on the desired results, (7) using MIS to support the SBM process, (8) developing problem-solving techniques, (9) devising evaluation methods, and (10) providing for a renewal cycle. The chapter also provides an SBM tactical planning responsibility chart. The development of MIS was described previously.

Defining School-Based Management

School-based management is both a structure and a process that involves representatives of employees, parents, citizens, and sometimes students in a local committee structure that is empowered to make decisions, at the local school building level, related to any or all of the following: (1) instruction, (2) budget, (3) personnel, (4) governance policies, and (5) any other matters that have been delegated to the local site level (Herman, 1990b).

SBM may be initiated by a variety of groups and individuals. In Kentucky and Texas this restructuring approach was mandated by the legislature (Herman & Herman, 1993). In Chicago and a few other cities, it was mandated by central authority. In other school districts, it sometimes is mandated by a board of education, superintendent of schools, or a principal; and often it is a voluntary effort by the teachers and principal of the local school, who initiate the SBM process and structure with the blessing of the superintendent and school board.

Regardless of how SBM was initiated, it must be a carefully planned long-term approach to restructuring. Careful planning must go into the specifics of: (1) the committee structure, (2) the areas and degrees of decision-making authority, (3) the local building by-laws and policies that must be developed as guides, (4) the training requirements of the participants, (5) the identification of needs (gaps or discrepancies between "what is" and "what should or could be") to be met, (6) the identification of desired results, (7) the development of an MIS, (8) the development of problem-solving techniques, and (9) the evaluation methods to be utilized to determine if the desired improvements are being met.

Once the threshold decision has been made to initiate and maintain the process and structure of SBM, the tactical planning cycle must be immediately initiated. It is tactical planning that determines how needs are to be identified and how tasks are to be completed to meet those identified needs.

These tactical planning steps can best be clarified by use of a model, such as that produced in Figure 7.1.

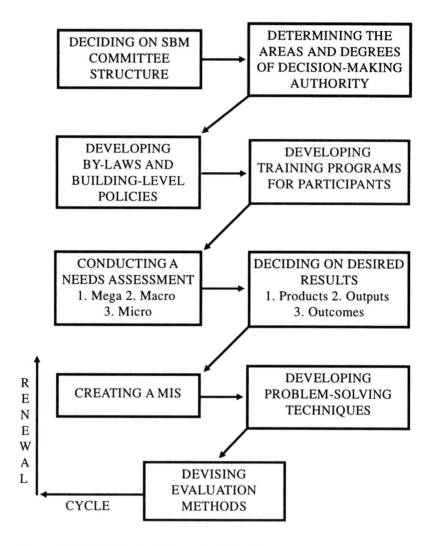

Figure 7.1. SBM Tactical Planning Model

Deciding on an SBM Committee Structure

The initial task to be accomplished by the person(s) responsible for initiating the SBM structure is to decide on the categories of stakeholders and the number of stakeholders to be included in each individual school's SBM steering committee (Crowson, 1992). Once this is decided, the SBM steering committee should be free to create subcommittees for any purposes that the SBM steering committee desires. The addition of numerous other persons on subcommittees has the purposes of distributing the detailed work and gaining ownership of the process, structure, and decisions by a much larger group of stakeholders than can be involved at the SBM steering committee level.

The membership of the steering committee should be represented by as many of the following groups as will be truly representative of the entire stakeholders of the school. Membership should definitely include: (1) parents, (2) students (if the members are initially willing to include them), (3) teachers, (4) classified employees, (5) the principal, and (6) other community members. The size of the committee will vary with the ultimate composition decided upon, but a general guideline is to create a steering committee that is large enough to be truly representative of all stakeholder groups and small enough to allow the business of the committee to be conducted in an efficient and effective manner.

Determining the Areas and Degrees of Local Decision-Making Authority

Once the committee membership is decided upon, the next task is to negotiate with the superintendent of schools, the board of education, and the central office administration which areas of decision making are to be given to the school building level and to determine which areas are to be retained by the central administration and board of education level and in which areas shared decisions are to be made (Herman, 1989d). It is also important to negotiate what degree of authority and responsibility is to be placed at the building and central office levels.

There are four major categories of decision making that must be addressed. They are those related to: (1) instruction, (2) finance, (3) personnel, and (4) governance. A few examples will illustrate the detailed possibilities.

Instruction-Related Decisions may allow each building to select varying instructional materials, varying lengths of time for each subject taught, and various methods of teaching. On the other hand, the overall curriculum balance and alignment may be controlled by the central level.

Finance-Related Decisions may allocate a stipulated amount of money per pupil, per teacher, or per standard (such as a teacher and 20 pupils). Within this allocation, all decisions can be made at the local school building level.

Personnel-Related Decisions could allow the SBM steering committee to select the teachers (with the agreement of the principal of the building) and select the principal (with the agreement of the superintendent of schools—when a vacancy occurs), and allow all classified and paraprofessional building-level employees to be selected by the central personnel office. Placement and evaluation will remain with administrators at the appropriate level, although the SBM steering committee could request a reevaluation at any time.

Governance-Related Decisions could grant the SBM steering committee the authority to decide on building-level policies and rules and regulations to implement those policies. In addition, the SBM steering committee could petition the board of education to exempt it from a district-level policy when the members feel that such a policy is negatively impacting the operation of their local school (Scholes, 1991).

Developing By-Laws and Building-Level Policies

The key to success in operating any organization is to place in writing clear by-laws and generate the minimum number of clearly worded policies that allows the organization to operate effectively and efficiently. Criteria for creating policies are two in number: (1) are they necessary to the smooth operation of the school, and (2) are they able to be monitored and equitably enforced.

By-laws are those details that allow the SBM steering committee and its subcommittees to operate in a meaningful and effective manner. By-laws will include such items as: (1) the membership of the committee(s) and how they are to be selected or elected; (2) the duties and responsibilities of the committee and its members; (3) the length of the term of service of the members, and whether they can serve more than one term; (4) the method of making decisions (by consensus or by majority vote); (5) the officers, if any, to be elected by the membership, and the duties and responsibilities of each officer; (6) the keeping of minutes of all decisions, and the distribution of the same; (7) the number and length of meetings; (8) the guide to be used in the conduct of the SBM steering committee's business (such as *Roberts' Rules of Order* or some variation thereof); and (9) any other operational details that are desired by the SBM steering committee's membership.

Developing Training Programs for Participants

A major error made by many school districts who decide to initiate SBM is assuming that a diverse representation of stakeholders who have not worked together, many of whom have not been given decision-making power over the school's operations, will automatically function well together. It is *crucial* that training sessions be provided before the SBM committee begins its work; it is also crucial that continuous training becomes an important agenda item for the committee; and it is crucial that as membership changes over time, new members are provided with training that will quickly bring them up to speed.

The basic types of training that should be provided all SBM steering committee members and all SBM subcommittee members include: (1) team building, (2) communication skills, (3) decision-making methods, (4) planning methods, (5) conflict resolution skills, (6) negotiation and consensus skills, and (7) any other training desired by the committee's members (Herman & Herman, 1993).

Conducting Mega, Macro, and Micro Needs Assessments

Once the committee structure has been decided upon, the decision-making areas of authority have been negotiated, the by-laws and building-level policies have been developed, and the necessary initial membership training has taken place, the SBM steering committee can get down to work on tasks designed to improve the operation of the school. At this juncture, the initial task is to conduct a needs assessment. This will eventually lead to the creation of a future preferred vision of "what should be" or "what could be" for the local school, its children, its employees, its parents, and the broader school community.

A need is a gap or discrepancy between "what is" and "what should or could be." There are three levels of needs that should be investigated by the SBM steering committee and its subcommittees. These levels include mega needs (those related to the general society to be served by the school), macro needs (those related to the entire school building's operations), and micro needs (those related to the sub-areas of the school, such as students or teachers, instruction or personnel, or the individual classroom or subject area).

Once the committees decide what should or could be the future vision, they can compare this vision to the existing state of affairs in their school. Thus, they can identify and prioritize the needs they wish to address to improve their school and its operations.

Deciding on the Desired Product, Output, and Outcome Results

Identifying and prioritizing the needs is an important first step in a school improvement agenda. The next important step is the determination of specific results to be achieved to meet the needs that have been identified. A few examples of student-level needs might well include: (1) decreasing the high school dropout rate by X%; (2) improving the reading scores, on a standardized test, by X for those students who are below grade level in the third grade; and (3) improving the social behavior of at-risk students, as measured by the severity and frequency of disciplinary incidents during a 6-month period, as compared to the previous 6 months. Of course each of these approaches would call for specific intervention program strategies to be devised and implemented, and the impact monitored.

A brief word of explanation about the three levels of results: products, outputs, and outcomes. As related to the student level, a product could be the receipt of a passing grade in a course, an output could be completing middle school, and an outcome might be becoming a productive citizen after graduation from high school. Productive citizenship could be defined as a person who produces more than he or she consumes.

Developing an SBM Planning Responsibility Chart

Once the needs assessment has been completed and the desired results identified, it is crucial to specify a comprehensive list of tasks to be completed to achieve the desired results related to each identified need. Once the tasks are identified, they should be listed in the chronological order to be completed, because without this task chronology a lot of time could be wasted and much inefficiency could occur. Then the person or persons responsible for completing each task must be identified, and the resources required to complete the assigned task identified and allocated. Finally, a target date for completing each task must be identified.

A simple responsibility chart will assist the SBM planners in their efforts. Such a chart is illustrated in Figure 7.2.

Once the task responsibilities are assigned, it is again important to develop an MIS. As described before, this MIS will not only collect, monitor, and array important decision-making data but will also serve as a continuous communication vehicle for all who are involved in the SBM process.

Creating an MIS

It does little good to identify needs and specify desired results if one does not devise an MIS to collect accurate data with which to measure the degree of achievement obtained by the intervention programs initiated to meet the identified needs. Again, at the student level, continuous data should be retrieved, arrayed, and analyzed to determine the effect of intervention programs on dropouts, reading scores, or unacceptable behavioral incidents. A well-designed MIS will not only provide the detailed hard (factual) and soft (opinions) data required to determine intervention programs' impacts but will also provide a wealth of information with which the school can communicate to all its stakeholders.

Task to Be Completed	Chronological Order	Person Responsible	Resources Required	Date to Be Completed

Figure 7.2. SBM Tactical Planning Responsibility Chart

Developing Problem-Solving Techniques

As the SBM committees attempt to design intervention programs to achieve the desired results relating to the needs that they identified, the members must be trained in problem-solving techniques. The basic structure of this training should include the following:

- Clearly identifying the actual problem
- Indicating the persons or groups involved in the problem
- Locating the possible causes of the problem
- Collecting hard and soft data about all persons or groups assumed to be involved and on all possible causes of the problem
- Narrowing the causes and persons involved until the picture is very accurate
- Developing alternative interventions to solve the problem
- Testing all alternative interventions
- Collecting accurate data to determine the effect of each intervention

- Agreeing that the problem is being solved and institutionalizing the intervention strategy or strategies that work

Devising Evaluation Methods

Evaluation methods should be determined before any action programs are put in place. The two basic types of evaluation that should be planned are formative and summative evaluations. Formative evaluations are those that are undertaken during the operation of the intervention program. Summative evaluations are those conducted after the program has been completed, at the end of a school year or at the end of some other predetermined time period. Formative evaluations are helpful in making important improvements during the intervention program's operation as errors or defects in the original plans are located. Summative evaluations are used to determine whether the intervention program has worked to a satisfactory level after the intervention has been completed or after a predetermined time period for measurement and evaluation.

Planning for a Renewal Cycle

Regardless of the activities of the SBM committees, there should always be an opportunity for change and renewal. Looking at a renewal cycle at a predetermined time period will allow the committees' membership to reflect on the entire work, address additional needs, assess the committees' and the programs' effectiveness and efficiency levels, and determine if meaningful changes will assist in helping their school and its stakeholders to be the best that it and they can be on the way to their preferred future vision.

Reminders

1. SBM must be considered to be long-term in nature and carefully planned.
2. Tactical planning should immediately follow the decision to implement SBM.

3. Keep SBM committees' membership as representative as possible.

4. Clarify the governance issues with respect to areas of decision making.

5. Ensure that clear SBM committee by-laws are written.

6. Provide appropriate training for all participants.

7. Plan for a renewal cycle.

Summary

Chapter 7 defined school-based management as a structure and a process that involve multiple stakeholders in a local committee empowered with decision-making authority at a local school level. As a long-term plan for restructuring, its implementation should be followed by the tactical planning cycle, which will help initiate and maintain SBM in schools. The SBM committee structure and the areas and degrees of decision-making authority must be designed with consideration given to broad participation and balanced autonomy.

The development of by-laws and building-level policies is critical for SBM success, as is the provision of training programs for the participants, particularly in group process and consensus skills. The strategic and tactical plan processes of needs assessments, identification and prioritization of needs, and the assignment of tasks were presented as SBM committee activities. Both the creation of an MIS to inform the decision-making activities of SBM and the focus on problem solving as a critical committee skill were described. Formative and summative evaluations and a plan for a renewal cycle to assess effectiveness and efficiency were also described.

Total Quality Management

PLANNING FOR TWENTY-FIRST
CENTURY LEADERSHIP

Chapter 8 relates basic Total Quality Management (TQM) concepts, applies them to education, and defines TQM in education. It is essential to be aware of the important issues related to change as a school district or a school building initiates and maintains TQM. A series of models identifies how TQM can fit into the overall planning responsibilities of a school district or school building. These models include: (1) an Overview Model, (2) a TQM Employee Subsystem Model, (3) a TQM Student Subsystem Model, (4) a TQM External Subsystem Model, (5) a TQM Strategic Planning Subsystem Model, (6) a TQM Tactical Planning Subsystem Model, and (7) a TQM Linkages between Products and Processes Model. As an umbrella structure and as a pervasive corporate or organizational mindset, TQM can both provide drive and ensure quality in the planning process, both strategically and tactically.

Laying the Foundation

There is a call in this country for improved quality in industry, health care, and education. Some of this force for improved quality is coming from business leaders who are having a difficult time competing with foreign nations—especially Japan and Germany. Some of this impetus is coming from the many people who possess no health insurance and from those individuals who feel they can no longer afford the accelerated costs of health care. Finally, educators are becoming more quality conscious because they are being criticized for producing inferior student products.

In education, attention to quality is being hastened by both a reduction of funds and the insistence of legislators and others calling for massive restructuring of the school systems of this country. The Kentucky Education Reform Act of 1990 is a dramatic example. Educators are bombarded on an almost daily basis with school-based management, choice initiatives, longer school days and years, and an ever-increasing number of suggestions about how to make the schools more effective in turning out quality products and quality services.

It is crucial that everyone become concerned about quality if we wish to retain our world leadership and provide a quality of life at least equivalent to that which we had not many years ago. Education is certainly a key ingredient in accomplishing these goals.

TQM is being implemented in more and more organizations each year. With some modifications to the model undertaken in the industrial and business sectors, TQM does offer an enticing restructuring opportunity for educators to explore (Herman, 1992). With the purpose of exploration in mind, this discussion will: (a) present some of the basic concepts of TQM, (b) develop TQM planning models that can be applied to education, and (c) elaborate upon the potential of the TQM models for use in planning in the field of education.

Basic TQM Concepts

The initial concepts for TQM originated with W. Edwards Deming's work in Japan during the recovery period following Japan's defeat during World War II. With a disastrous condition existing, Japan's leaders decided to employ Dr. Deming as a consultant to revitalize their industries. The result is evident, as Japan has overtaken the United States in many areas.

Dr. Deming has stated his basic concepts into 14 points that are cited by numerous authors (Butterfield, 1991; Melvin, 1991; Milakovich, 1990; Scherkenbach, 1991; Sui-Runyan & Hart, 1992). His 14 points are:

- Create a constancy of purpose toward improvement of product and service.
- Adopt a new philosophy.
- Cease dependence on mass inspection.
- End the practice of awarding business on the basis of price tag alone.
- Improve constantly and forever the system of production and service.
- Institute modern methods of training.
- Institute leadership.
- Drive out fear so that everyone may work effectively for the organization.
- Break down barriers between staff areas.
- Eliminate arbitrary numerical goals, slogans, and targets.
- Eliminate work standards and numerical quotas.
- Remove barriers that rob employees of their pride in workmanship.
- Institute a vigorous program of education and retraining.
- Take actions to accomplish the transformation.

In addition to Deming's influential points, another significant influence took place in 1987, when the United States Congress established the Malcolm Baldridge National Quality Award (Paton, 1991). This much-desired and very competitive award is given to a few very select organizations each year. In fact, each year two awards are given in each of the three categories of manufacturing, service, and small business. In deciding on the award winners, "Examiners scrutinize seven areas: (1) leadership, (2) information and analysis, (3) planning, (4) human resource use, (5) quality assurance of products and services, (6) quality results, and (7) customer satisfaction" (Paton, 1991, p. 38).

There are numerous definitions offered for the term *Total Quality Management*. For example, Jablonski (1991) defines it as: "A cooperative form of doing business that relies on the talents and capabilities of both labor and management to continually improve quality and productivity using teams" (p. 4). Vincoli (1991) defines TQM: "Total Quality Management is a customer-focused, strategic and systematic approach to continuous performance improvement" (p. 28).

Other sources of information on TQM offer additional elements as basic concepts. Some of the most significant ones that can potentially influence the type of TQM modifications required for a good fit in the educational environment include the following:

> Many good things flow from the energetic pursuit of Total Quality. A quality campaign gets attention and resources from senior management. It demands cross-functional co-operation. It forces people at all levels to shift attention from their bosses to their customers. And it exposes hidden pockets of waste, inefficiency and communication break-downs. (McLagan, 1991, p. 31)

> Before the word "customer" usually referred to someone outside the organization, a person someone else worried about. TQM views customers in a different light: "the customer is the person who receives my work as input for his or her work. The next person in the work process is my customer, and I must meet his or her requirements." (Ferketish, 1991, p. 57)

> To improve a process, you have to change parts of it. These parts are categorized as inputs, transformations and outputs. The subparts of transformation are people, equipment, materials, and environment. The transformation produces a value-added output. (Ammon & Plato, 1991)

> The team's first job is to define the parts of the process that affect the issue being addressed. Then they identify the

process stakeholders and find out what the stakeholders require in terms of process performance. This is a critical step, since the stakeholders are the ultimate judges of how well a process performs. Next, the team develops indicators that measure process performance and write out stakeholder requirements in these terms. They then collect and analyze data on actual performance and compare it to requirements. (Ammon & Plato, 1991)

TQM involves six basic principles: (1) customer focus, (2) focus on the process as well as the results, (3) prevention versus inspection, (4) mobilizing expertise of the workforce, (5) fact-based decision making, and (6) feedback. (Jablonski, 1991)

"Give me the data" is the expression you hear in every important discussion and evaluation at Toyota. And this aspect of management is—despite all our talk about improvement—what we school leaders overlook. Only about 20 percent of what we regard as most valuable to our students is measured by standardized tests. (Wilson & Schmoker, 1992)

Total Quality Management is a customer-focused, strategy-driven approach that makes new and profound demands on every organization.
- Quality is a personal obligation of everyone, not just the responsibility of "that" department.
- Products and services must meet or exceed customer expectations.
- Quality demands a proactive culture within the organization that addresses quality on both the source and delivery ends of the supply chain.
- Adversarial relationships are replaced by partnerships with employees, suppliers, and customers.
- The focus is on continuous improvement plus major step function improvements.
- Employees at all levels must be empowered to make decisions that allow them to provide superior quality and service.

–   Quality is recognized as a journey rather than a destination. Its only goal is to exceed the customer's expectations. (Steingraber, 1991)

TQM is often described as a "journey to excellence" since it is an approach that envisions a long-range effort with many major goals.

The Federal Quality Institute identifies several key factors that determine successful quality efforts and shape the process:

- top management support;
- customer focus;
- long-term strategic planning;
- employee training and recognition;
- employee empowerment and teamwork;
- measurement and analysis of products and processes; and
- quality assurance. (Hyde, 1990-1991)

Using the basics previously reviewed, it is reasonable to now turn to the possible use of TQM within the field of education. This can be quickly accomplished by arriving at a simple listing of the concepts that seem to most closely fit the educational environment and from which application models can be derived.

TQM Concepts Applied to Education

The following concepts are foundational beacons for those who wish to arrive at applications of TQM for their educational organizations, particularly in the planning function:

- The school district's and individual school's mission must focus on a vision, policies, and strategic goals that lead to the delivery of high-quality services and products to all customers.
- Educational customers include all internal (students and employees) as well as all external (parents, residents, and other agencies that interact with the schools) stakeholders.

- TQM should focus on the processes that are designed to continuously produce quality products at each step and to all customers.

- TQM has a value-added dimension, in that every step of the process will lead to an improved output, and quality is added to each step.

- Ultimately, customers define quality standards, and satisfaction of customers is only gained through meeting or exceeding these standards.

- Extensive two-way communications with all stakeholders is required to define the quality specifications to be used by the schools or school districts.

- TQM involves a systems approach, and TQM school districts' or school buildings' decision makers should constantly improve the quality of their systems or processes.

- Employees are empowered through communication, training, and encouraging leadership. Many times problemsolving teams are utilized to remove glitches in the systems or processes.

- Training is continuously required for management, employees, and suppliers to make certain that they are constantly attentive to improvement in the quality of the products and services.

- Constancy of measurement, not just limited to standardized test scores, is crucial to quality assurance.

- TQM is about change, and change involves causing changes in behaviors.

- School districts and schools that implement TQM must realize that it will cause changes, and that these changes could be so dramatic as to ultimately change the culture of the school districts and schools that comprise them.

- To maintain this desired cultural state, school districts and schools will have to scan the external and internal environments to assess the potential impacts of internal and external variables that continuously keep changing. This must be done in order to effectively develop strategic and tactical plans to deal with these variables.

- For TQM to be seriously considered, transformational leadership must be present. Transformational leaders are those individuals who are visionaries driven by long-term goals to achieve the preferred future quality vision for their schools and school districts.

- TQM school districts and individual school buildings possess an environment—a learning climate—that emanates from a culture that speaks directly and constantly to the issue of quality. If this does not take place, the hoped-for quality school district or school building will become next year's major failure. If successfully done, quality will permeate every nook and cranny, as well as the thoughts of every stakeholder within the schools and those who have direct dealings with the schools.

- Finally, it must be emphasized that TQM is not a quick fix. Rather, it is a long-term strategic goal that can be accomplished only by much hard and devoted labor by stakeholders who believe and accept ownership for a successful quality infusion into the schools.

Now that the basic concepts have been discussed, it is time to spell out the definition to be used when applying TQM to the educational planning environment. Having the definition at hand, a few words about change must be emphasized, and then the task of developing models can take place.

Definition of TQM

Total Quality Management is a:

- *Philosophy* that believes that both internal and external customers are to be provided with an ever-improving quality of products and services, and one that believes in the utilization of feedback from these customers to develop the specifications of the quality levels to be achieved for each product and each service, in other words, to inform the planning process.

- *Goal* that states that each product or service delivered to each category of customer (student, external customer, and employee), and all activities or milestones leading to that final product or service, shall be of the highest quality they can be.
- *Process* that accepts feedback from all stakeholders to define the qualitative level and the products and services specifications to be met; and it utilizes empowered and well-trained employees, within a systems structure, to develop products or services at each value-added juncture that will ultimately result in the delivery of those high-quality products and services in a manner that will cause maximum customer satisfaction.

Change and TQM

TQM involves change, and change comes hard to many individuals. There are three major types of change that affect the employees of a school district or a school building.

Optional Change is the preferred method when groups of employees initiate and support the change. This type of change is not mandated by the principal, superintendent, or school board. This type of change is usually very successful because the employees who must manage it are the ones who initiated the change.

Incremental Change is preferred when everything is working well but stakeholders agree that minor changes can be made to improve the educational quality.

Transformational Change is the only rational choice when a school or a school district is not operating at a satisfactory level of quality of service, or it is not producing satisfactorily educated youngsters. Transformational change is required when an organization must modify its structures and processes to meet its customers' expectations.

TQM involves transformational change, which, when completed, will redesign the current planning structures and processes utilized in the school district and/or the school building. Ultimately, the successful implementation of TQM will lead to a new organizational culture that will produce high-quality results and a great degree of customer satisfaction.

A series of models will illustrate how TQM can operate within an educational planning environment. Figure 8.1 presents the Overview Model, and the subsequent six figures illustrate the application of TQM to the subareas of operational planning in a school district or school building.

Models and Potential Usages of TQM in the Field of Education

Figure 8.1 presents the Overview TQM Model. It begins with a commitment to quality and customer satisfaction and moves through the steps of: (1) commitment, (2) needs assessment, (3) quality specifications, (4) strategic plans, (5) tactical plans, (6) formative and summative assessments, and (7) measurement and feedback recycling.

Following the sequence of Figure 8.1, it is clear that once the very important consensus commitment by the internal and external stakeholders is for quality and customer satisfaction, the operational planning steps can be initiated. Once this commitment is made, the following steps and processes are required:

1. A *needs assessment* must be conducted with the three customer groups of students, employees, and parents and community members all being assessed as to their perceived needs. A need can be defined as a gap or discrepancy between "what should or could be" and "what is" currently in place. The needs identified by the students, external stakeholders and customers, and employees should be carefully identified and evaluated. They then become the criteria upon which the decision makers and planners can devise strategic and tactical plans to meet the valid identified needs.

For each need, quality specifications must be developed. These quality specifications should cover both the services and the products to be delivered to the customers. They should be developed for each of the functional areas of the school or school district (administration, personnel, instruction, business, and support services), for each grade level offered in the school or the district, for

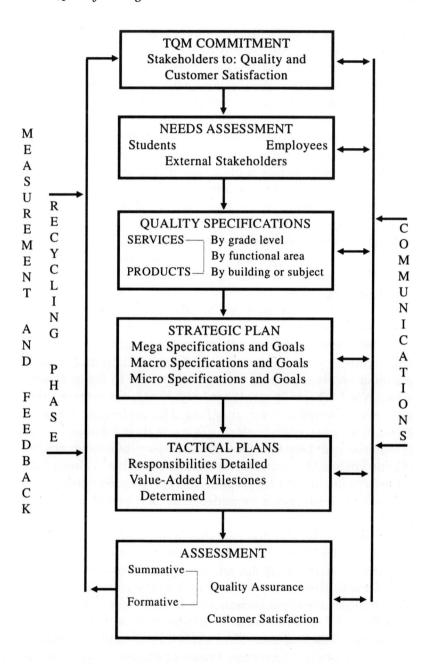

Figure 8.1. TQM Model for School Districts

each instructional and support program offered, for each school building or site within the district, and for each subject area offered within the school or school district.

2. Once the quality specifications have been fine-tuned, *strategic plans* should be developed. Strategic planning in education, as in other organizational areas, involves three levels: mega, macro, and micro planning. Mega specifications are those that relate to the broader society and the external environment. Macro specifications refer to those that apply to the total school district. Micro specifications are those that relate to the individual school building, a department, a grade level, an individual program, or a specific functional area. These three types of specifications are utilized as the bases for developing strategic goals. Strategic goals are long-term goals designed to achieve the vision of the "what should be" future state of all elements that exist in a school or a school district.

3. When the strategic plans are finalized, the planners and decision makers can move on to the task of developing *tactical plans*. Tactical plans represent the *hows* (ways to achieve the goals), while strategic plans represent the *whats* (the actual goals). Tactical planning involves arriving at specific answers to the questions: Why? Who? Where? What? When? and How? When these questions are answered in detail, they lead to the immediate actions to be taken to achieve the strategic goals and their subobjectives. It is important not only that the detailed responsibilities for achieving the goals and objectives are clear but also that value-added (improved quality at each step) milestones are predetermined to measure the level of quality achieved at each step of the tactical plans.

4. Once the tactical plans are placed into operation, an *assessment* of the degree of achievement reached should be made. Assessments should be conducted during the operational stage of each tactical plan to determine if mid-course corrections are required. These in-process corrections are based upon formative assessments. A final assessment should be made at the end of the tactical plan. This final assessment is called a summative assessment.

5. Throughout all the steps, *two-way* clear and concise *communications* must be conducted if successful implementation of TQM

is to be maximized. It is absolutely crucial that all stakeholders know the steps being taken to achieve the strategic goals and objectives, and it is important that communications are two-way communications. All stakeholders must have opportunities to provide inputs to the people who are managing the strategic and tactical planning stages of the model. Change is difficult, and TQM is a dramatic structural change, which, if successfully implemented, will ultimately change the structures, processes, and cultures of a school or a school district. It is evolutionary, not revolutionary, in nature and it depends on a critical mass of stakeholders claiming ownership.

6. Finally, it is practically impossible to cause a dramatic change that will be 100% successful upon its initial implementation. Therefore, the model insists upon a *recycling phase* that mandates continuous measurement and feedback. This recycling phase is used to determine the gaps between *what is* and *what was* intended by the strategic and tactical plans. In other words, the recycling stage is used whenever the strategic and tactical plans do not coincide with the desired results or do not meet the quality level desired in the quality specifications that were developed for both the areas of services and the products to be delivered to each group of customers.

Since the Overview TQM Model has been defined, it is time to turn to the subset models that will further explain the TQM planning structures and processes and their fit to the educational environment. The initial subset model is related to the employees of the school or the school district.

The TQM Employee Subsystem Model, as presented in Figure 8.2, involves four discrete steps and it ends with a measurement and feedback recycling phase that serves the purpose of making any required modifications in the original planning or operational phase.

To make TQM fully operational and sustainable, the initial step is the *selection of employees* who believe in: (1) the school's and/or school district's TQM culture; (2) collaborative ways of working, planning, and making decisions; (3) the goal of delivering quality services and products to all customers; and (4) satisfying, to the highest degree possible, all categories of the school's and/or school district's customers.

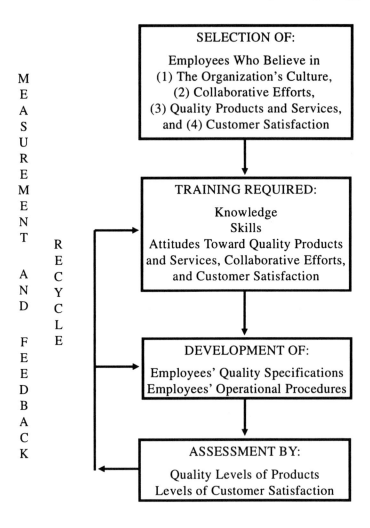

Figure 8.2. TQM Employee Subsystem Model

Once the employees who believe in TQM are on board, the next step is *providing extensive training* to all new and experienced employees relating to the knowledge, attitudes, and skills required to provide quality products and services to all categories of the school's and/or school district's customers.

Once employees who believe in the TQM culture are hired and trained, they can be solicited to assist in *developing quality specifications* for all the products and services to be provided; and they can develop and carry on the tactical plans (operational procedures) that are necessary to develop the products and services that meet the qualitative levels specified.

Next, the *tactical plans must be assessed* to determine the qualitative levels achieved for the products produced and for the levels of customer satisfaction with the services provided.

Finally, there is a continuing requirement of measurement and feedback. This comprises the *recycling phase* of the model and is required if corrections are to be made in any deficiencies detected in the outputs of services or products. The recycling might well take place at either the training level or the specifications level or both.

The TQM Student Subsystem, illustrated in Figure 8.3, also involves four basic steps, with a measurement and feedback recycling phase added.

The TQM Student Subsystem steps are:

- *Determining the outcome-based qualitative level* specifications expected of the groups of students related to their expected qualitative levels of achievement.
- *Developing the individual student's qualitative level* of achievement specifications.
- *Providing the instructional deliverables and the technological support systems* required to assist the students to achieve at or above the expected and specified qualitative levels.
- *Assessing the qualitative level achieved* by each student and by each group of students. Assessments of students will involve the applications of *knowledge* (cognitive, affective, and psychomotor), the applications of *skills*, and the applications of *attitudes*.
- *Conducting the measurement and feedback* necessary to ensure meaningful modifications in structure, specifications, and process during the recycling phase. If the qualitative

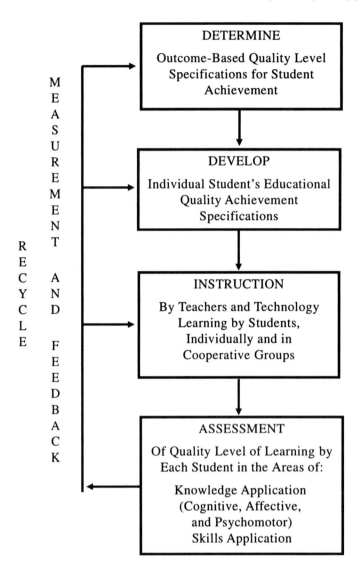

Figure 8.3. TQM Student Subsystem

level expected and specified is not achieved, there will be
a recycling to modify the development and/or the instructional steps of the model.

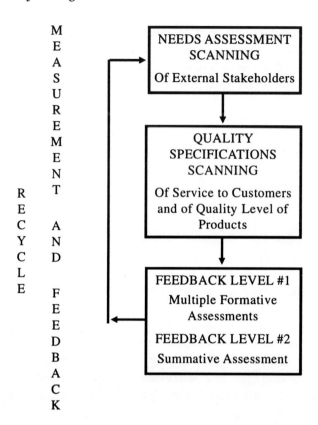

Figure 8.4. TQM External Environmental Subsystem

Figure 8.4, the External Subsystem, also involves four similar steps and a recycling phase.

The initial step for this subsystem is that of conducting a *needs assessment* of the external customers (stakeholders). A need is a gap or discrepancy between "what should or could be" in the future (a preferred future scenario) and "what is" currently in existence. Once these external needs are clearly identified, step 2, that of developing *quality specifications* for both the services and products that were identified by the needs assessment activities, has to be completed.

Step 3 involves providing continuous, accurate and complete feedback during the *formative stage* of this subsystem's operations.

During this stage, the external customers provide input during the operation of the tactical plans. These inputs may cause the decision makers and those responsible for managing the tactical plans to decide to make modifications during the operational stage of the tactical plans.

The fourth step in this subsystem involves gathering feedback information from the external customers at the end of the operational activities. This *summative feedback* may cause the strategic and tactical managers and planners to modify and/or restructure what has been done as the process is renewed.

Once step 4 has been completed, a *recycling stage* is activated. During this stage, structures and processes may be deleted, modified, or added to because of: (a) the changing need of the customers over time, (b) requirements to repair identified quality deficits, and/or (c) a desire to reach new and higher-quality specifications for products and/or services to be delivered to the external environment.

As we move to comprehensive strategic planning, which is long-term planning to achieve a future vision of what should or could be, viewing Figure 8.5 will illustrate this very important TQM Strategic Planning Subsystem Model.

The initial step in the Strategic Planning Process Subsystem Model involves the activity of *identifying the needs* (discrepancies between "what is" and "what should or could be") for the three customer levels served by the school and/or school district. These three groups of very crucial customers are: (1) external customers, (2) employee customers, and (3) student customers. Once the needs of the three levels of customers are determined, a school and/or a school district vision of the preferred future can be developed during the planning process. This *preferred future vision* within a TQM organization should include, as a minimum, the following elements:

- A high level of customer satisfaction.
- A system of continuous and accurate two-way communications and feedback with all three categories of customers.

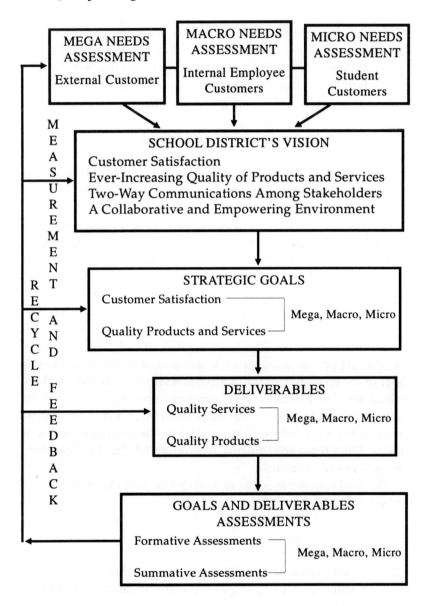

Figure 8.5. TQM Strategic Planning Process Subsystem Model

- A collaborative and empowering environment for all categories of the school's or school district's customers, but this type of environment for students is especially important for students and employees.

- A constant desire and goal to produce an ever-increasing quality of both products and services to the school's and/or school district's three categories of customers.

Once the preferred future vision for the school and/or school district has been determined and consensus reached upon it, the next planning step of deciding upon *strategic goals* can be activated. These goals should definitely include goals related to a very high degree of all categories of customer satisfaction with both the products produced and the services provided by the schools. Once the strategic goals have been formulated, the deliverables related to quality services and quality products must be devised.

After the deliverables have been decided upon and put into operation, *formative (in-process) assessments* have to be frequently taken. Once the deliverables have reached an end point, a *summative (after the process is completed) assessment* must be conducted. If either of the formative or summative assessments displays deficits in the desired qualitative level of services or products to any of the three groups of customers, the items must be recycled for adjustments at the most appropriate step(s) in the strategic planning process. Once these adjustments are completed, the strategic planning process can continue.

The final subsystem is that of the TQM Tactical Planning Process Subsystem (see Figure 8.6).

The steps of the TQM Tactical Planning Process Subsystem include the following:

- A *needs assessment* that includes both the products (desired results) and the processes (means to reach the desired results).

- *Tactical objectives* that clearly and specifically define the qualitative levels desired for each service and each product to be delivered to all three categories of customers.

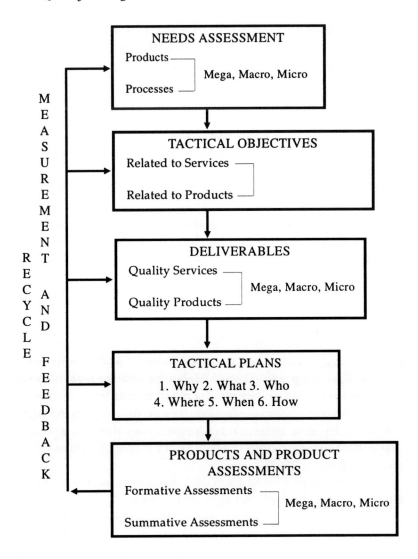

Figure 8.6. TQM Tactical Planning Process Subsystem

- *Deliverables* (specifics) for both services and products.
- *Tactical plans* that are developed and operationalized in a manner to achieve the tactical objectives. These plans are

designed in a manner to answer the detailed questions of: Why? What? Who? Where? When? and How?

• *Product and process assessment* of each tactical plan for each of the three groups of customers (external, student, and employee) are conducted and, based upon the assessment results, a recycling of any of the previous steps will take place for any area and for any customer category where quality deficits in products or services are identified.

Before leaving this discussion of how TQM can best fit educational planning, and having reviewed the TQM Model and all of its subsystems models in some detail, it is important to once again emphasize the requirement of a close, accurate, and continuous linkage between the process and product elements of TQM. These linkages are clarified in Figure 8.7.

Concluding Statements

TQM has much to offer individual school's or school district's planners and decision makers, stakeholders, and customers. If done well, it can provide both a higher qualitative level of products, processes, and services and a much higher level of internal and external customer satisfaction. It is neither a quick fix nor a revolutionary idea. Indeed, it is a long-term evolutionary process that will ultimately change the culture of the school and/or school district (Herman, 1993).

TQM can engulf, build upon, and strengthen two other change efforts that are currently being touted in education. It can utilize the effective schools research as cornerstone goals, and it can capitalize on the school-based management empowerment process to develop ownership and the desire to emphasize the quality in TQM (Herman, in press).

Reminders

1. Emphasize the TQM concepts of high-quality services and products, internal and external customer focus, and the value-added dimension as particular educational applications.

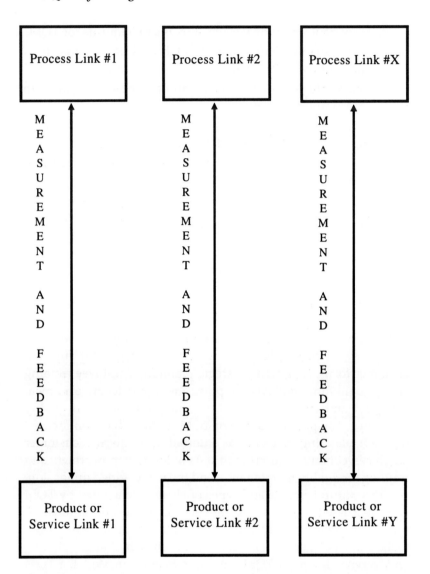

Figure 8.7. TQM Systems Model: Linkages Between Process and Product

2. View transformational leadership as a prerequisite for TQM.

3. The systemic change that TQM brings about must be a constant consideration.

4. The strategic and tactical planning process is critical to TQM implementation.

5. Maintain constant communications with stakeholders during the implementation of TQM.

6. Continue measurement and feedback during the recycling phase.

7. The subsystems of TQM are integral to the process and illustrate the linkages between the product and process elements.

Summary

Chapter 8 related basic TQM concepts in a larger societal and cultural sense and as applied to educational planning. The historical origins were described, and numerous definitions were offered. Key elements identified were top management support, customer focus, long-term strategic planning, employee training and recognition, employee empowerment and teamwork, measurement and analysis of products and processes, and quality assurance. The possible usage of TQM within education focused on such planning elements as internal and external customer emphasis, communications with stakeholders, empowerment and training for quality maintenance, and the value-added dimension.

The cultural change and types of change demanded by TQM were discussed: optional, incremental, and transformational. A series of models was presented to illustrate the application of TQM to the planning operational sub-areas of a school building, including an Overview Model, a TQM Employee Subsystem Model, a TQM Student Subsystem Model, a TQM External Subsystem Model, a TQM Strategic Planning Subsystem Model, a TQM Tactical Planning Subsystem Model, and a TQM Linkages Between Products and Processes Model. The strategic and tactical planning processes were interwoven throughout the subsystems; the linkage between them and TQM is critical to product and process quality.

9 Tying It All Together

PLANNING, LEADERSHIP, AND CHANGE

Chapter 9 is devoted to clarifying the linkages between and among strategic and tactical thinking, planning, managing, and evaluating. It stresses the interdependence of planning, leadership, and change.

Linkages Between Tactical and Strategic Thinking, Planning, Managing, and Evaluating

If a school district or an individual school is to be transformationally and systemically changed; and if the change is to create a culture which promotes dramatic changes in the structures, processes, and attitudes which exist, it has a much better opportunity to do these things if it unifies and blends the separate approaches into one coordinated and complementary approach to transformational change and to a new systemic organizational culture. (Herman, 1993, p. 36)

The linkages of the tactical and strategic planning processes into one holistic and systemic change structure and process have been stressed throughout the chapters in this book (Kaufman & Herman,

1991b). Deliberate connections, cumulative applications, and a spiral of planning strategies and skills have characterized the thrust of the information provided.

Once the planners and decision makers feel that the district or school is sufficiently ready to attempt systemic, transformational change, they can address the task of integrating the various programs of SBM, effective schools, and strategic and tactical planning into a holistic structure to achieve planning for true systemic change (Herman & Herman, 1993). SBM fits within the concepts of strategic and tactical planning in that it provides the ideal decision-making vehicle for the processes. It was suggested that to create a preferred future vision for a school district or school building a stakeholders' school-based management council be utilized. Strategic goals can be operationally determined by using the effective school correlates in combination with an assessment of needs that has been garnered from conducting an internal and external scanning exercise. Finally, it was suggested throughout the book that tactical plans (the how-to) utilize procedures to achieve the strategic goals and objectives.

Reviewing the key concepts of SBM, effective schools, and strategic and tactical planning, we find that a complementary approach of these concepts will allow the development of a holistic approach to positive systemic and transformational planning and change in schools. These key concepts are displayed in Figure 9.1.

Using the strategic and tactical planning concepts as the basic structure, it is possible to combine the concepts of SBM and effective schools with the planning concepts. It is also clear that each step of the strategic and tactical planning structure can accommodate the concepts of SBM and effective schools. Although some steps in the planning structures have stronger implications than others for the integration of SBM and effective schools into a holistic approach, it is clear that strong evidence exists in the commonality of the concepts of:

- Empowered stakeholders
- Needs assessment
- Strategic goals

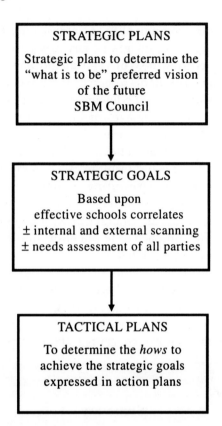

Figure 9.1. Connecting Effective Schools Research, Strategic and Tactical Planning, and School-Based Management

- Strategic objectives
- Action programs
- Data collection and feedback
- Planning
- Strong leadership
- Collaborative decision making
- Climate conducive to support

Considering the commonality of components, it is clear that it is desirable to plan as an integrated structure, rather than taking each of the restructuring ideas of: (1) strategic planning, (2) tactical planning, (3) effective schools research, and (4) school-based management as independent methodologies to attempt school improvement. If more than one of these restructuring efforts is attempted in the same school district or same school building, without integrating them into a single approach effort, conflict between the various restructuring methods could result in much damage. In addition, if these initial efforts at restructuring are unsuccessful because of the lack of coordination between or among the various methods, it will create substantial stakeholder unwillingness to accept another restructuring approach or to put effort into any planning or change strategy (Herman, 1993).

Reviewing the key concepts of SBM, effective schools, and strategic and tactical planning, there is a complementary approach of these concepts which creates an integrated and holistic approach to planning for positive systemic and transformational change in schools. The key concepts to be incorporated are displayed in Table 9.1.

Summary

This book has shared information about change and leaders and has provided a wide variety of practical planning tools designed to assist educational leaders in their responsibility to develop and maintain successful schools. In its design for use as a day-to-day reference guidebook for those educational leaders who are responsible for and accountable to direct change that improves the operations and outputs of their school districts and their school buildings, it has attempted to combine the larger perspective and concept of strategic, long-term planning with a vision with the shop-floor and practitioner-friendly strategies to accomplish that aspiration.

Key points to successfully implementing and maintaining an integrated planning process for both yearly and long-term transformational change are many, but the main ones include the following:

TABLE 9.1 Interface Between Key Concepts and Planning Steps

Planning Steps	*Key Concepts*
STRATEGIC PLAN	**EFFECTIVE SCHOOLS**
A. Vision	1. Vision of preferred future
B. Beliefs and Values	2. Instructional leadership
C. External and Internal Scanning	3. Parent and community involvement
D. Critical Success Factors	4. Conductive climate
E. Needs Assessment	5. Emphasis on basic skills
F. Mission	6. Data collection and feedback
G. SWOT Analysis	
H. Strategic Goals	7. Mastery
I. Specific Objectives for Goals	**SCHOOL-BASED MANAGEMENT**
J. Evaluate and Recycle	
	1. Empowerment to the school site
TACTICAL PLAN	2. Stakeholders' involvement in decision making
K. Decision Rules to Determine Priorities	3. Collaborative decision making
L. Action Plans:	4. Conducive support climate
1. Brainstorm	
2. Force Field Analysis	
3. Cost/Benefit Analysis	
4. Select Best Alternative	
5. Allocate Resources and Operate Plans	
M. Evaluate and Recycle	

- Stakeholders must be involved in the process and in the decisions.
- Strategic and the corresponding operational (tactical) plans must be identified and carried out by the decision makers

and the managers of change; and these plans must be aligned.

- A vision, goals, and objectives that spell out the various levels of desired results must be clear and understood by all.
- Data must be collected and analyzed, and feedback must be provided to the decision makers and to the managers of change so that they make improvements and modifications as required over time.
- Employees and a critical mass of other stakeholders must believe in the preferred future vision for the school district and its constituent schools, and they must accept ownership of the strategic goals, specific objectives, and tactical plans that are designed to achieve the preferred future vision.
- The preferred future vision must be one that includes continuous improvement of the quality of the products and services of the school district and its constituent schools. Once this result is attained, the district will witness a mass of satisfied internal and external customers. (Herman, 1993)

What has been described in this text is not a quick fix and foolproof method of improving schools. It is, however, a long-term planning approach that integrates various planning models, strategies, and current restructuring ideas into an approach to school improvement, which holds great promise for attaining the ultimate goals of producing high-quality graduates who will become productive citizens and of implementing quality planning processes that will provide all of the districts' schools with direction and impetus toward success, year after year.

Glossary

Accountability: The requirement to answer for the results of professional effort, usually expressed and measured as student achievement and outcomes and institutional effectiveness.

Action Plan: An operational plan that clearly and comprehensively answers the questions of Why, What, How, When, Who, and Where as these questions apply to a specific set of tasks and procedures designed to achieve an objective.

Alternate Futuring: The process of deciding a variety of possible futures for an organization. Each alternate can then be analyzed for its probability and its desirability.

Brainstorming: A solution-generating activity where all the planners generate as many ideas as possible over a short time frame, with no accompanying discussion.

Cost/Benefit Analysis: A procedure to determine the value of what is achieved by the cost of implementing proposed planning actions.

Critical Path Method (CPM):   A type of critical path analysis planning used when a planned project, such as the construction of an elementary school with a standard type of district K-5 architecture, has very well-known subtasks and for which the completion time estimates are reasonably well known.

Critical Success Factors (CSF):   Those few factors that are determined to be vital for development and maintenance of a high-quality organization. They provide priorities that assist in resource allocations and in determining information requirements.

Decentralization: Dispersion or distribution of educational functions and authority from a central power level to regional or local school authorities.

Decision Rules: Rules that determine which objective should be given priority attention.

Delegation: This involves the actual transfer of decision-making authority to a lower level in the hierarchy; it must, however, be executed within a firm policy framework.

Delphi: A structured process for achieving consensus without the requirement of face-to-face contact by the participants. Originally designed to solicit opinions about the future from experts, it can also be used as a decision-making technique for strategic and tactical planning stakeholders' groups.

Disaggregation: To break down the hard and soft data in a school's MIS system into a more detailed display in order to discern trends among gender, ethnic group, socioeconomic status, or programmatic participation.

Effective Schools Research: Cluster of characteristics correlated to school effectiveness, usually described as instructional leadership; clear and focused mission; an emphasis on instruction; safe and orderly school climate; monitoring and measuring of achievement; time devoted to learning; and parent and community support.

Empowerment: A fundamental transfer of authority, usually to teachers or other professionals within a school system; the process of allowing employees to make decisions related to assigned work tasks, involving them in the creation of ways to maintain a productive and satisfying work environment and in day-to-day problem solving and decision making.

External Scanning: The activity of collecting and monitoring data from the external environment in which the organization (school district or university) exists, for the purpose of identifying trends over time that can be utilized to assist in planning strategies for the future.

Fishbowl Technique: A consensus technique whereby a group of representative spokespersons is selected from broader groups to discuss and negotiate points that will lead to consensus, while the larger membership observes the dialogue.

Focus Groups: Comprised of employees and management, they are usually assembled to deal with a specific problem that is facing the school district. Focus groups usually meet for very short periods of time; and the task of a focus group is usually one of isolating a problem, analyzing the variables that impact the problem, and brainstorming possible solutions.

Force Field Analysis: A systematic procedure for identifying possible tactics to be used in achieving an action plan; the analysis focuses on a comparison of the constraining and supporting forces.

Governance: Authoritative direction or control within a school district or within a state or regional educational structure.

Hard Data: Performance or other data that are independently verifiable.

Human Resource Development: It involves all activities within the educational organization or school district with the potential of having a positive or a negative effect on the people who work within the school district.

Incremental Change: A type of change whereby the stakeholders agree that minor changes will assist in improving the current operations to an even greater degree; change by degrees.

Internal Scanning: The activity of collecting and monitoring data from within the internal environment of the organization (school district or university) for the purpose of identifying trends over time that assist in planning strategies for the future.

Issue Papers: Planning or problem-solving technique that uses ideas created by brainstorming, the array of supporting and restraining factors generated by force field analysis, and detailed action plans; the specific set of tasks and procedures designed to achieve one or more of the objectives of the strategic plan. It is a culminating type of activity, creating a clarified planning proposal or alternative as an outcome of the preceding processes.

Macro-Level Planning: Strategic planning that begins with beliefs about the total organization as its goal.

Management by Objectives (MBO):   A strategy of planning to attain improved results in managerial actions, seeking to maximize organizational efficiency while meeting the needs of participants.

Management Information System (MIS):   A formal data system established to collect and disseminate information to be used by those individuals who are given the responsibility for decision making and strategic planning.

Mega-Level Planning: Planning that begins with beliefs about society as its goal.

Micro-Level Planning: Strategic planning that begins with beliefs about a subgroup within the total organization.

Mission: The overall job to be done to meet the identified and documented needs; a statement of "Where are we headed?" and "How will we know when we have arrived?"

Mission Statement: The intentions about what is to be accomplished. A mission statement is often inspirational while providing general direction.

Narrow and Wide Lens Tactical Planning: Planning methods that are distinguished by a difference in focus; the targeting of a specific, individual problem or need.

Needs: Discrepancies between "what is" and "what could be" or "what should be" in strategic planning.

Needs Assessments: Instruments or processes that identify the needs during the planning process, place them in order of priority, and select those to be reduced or eliminated.

Nominal Group Technique: A structured process devised to stimulate new ideas and to arrive at consensus. It encourages all to participate, it spotlights discussions on specific questions, and it eventually reaches consensus by a series of voting exercises.

Optional Change: A type of change whereby key groups of employees initiate the change.

Organizational Development: This involves the maintenance and improvement of the total school district and all its components.

Outcomes: The social impacts and payoffs of planning results for society.

Participation: The process whereby subordinates have more input into a decision.

Polling: A structured process involving representative individuals that indicates their preferences or predictions. This can be done by telephone interviews, face-to-face interviews, or a mail opinionnaire. The results of the polling provide information that assists the strategic planner in devising strategies.

Preferred Futuring: The process of selecting the most desired future from the group of alternate futures that have been developed. This preferred future becomes the cornerstone for the organization's vision.

Professionalization: The enlargement of teacher discretion in making decisions, both in the immediate workplace and in the larger context of school and system.

Program Evaluation Review Technique (PERT):   A network-based tool for planning, such as planning the implementation of an educational system. This technique programs each detailed task and activity along an identified time line, thus providing a blueprint for displaying events to be accomplished and the person(s) responsible for carrying out the activity within the time frame indicated.

Restructuring: A concept that encompasses the need to rethink educational mission in view of changing conditions and imperatives; to exchange traditional forms of schooling and professional practice for new pedagogical and organizational structures.

Scenario: A written narrative describing a future. This technique can be helpful if a variety of experts are asked to develop a future scenario for the organization; those consensus elements are identified and redistributed to the experts for additional comments; and this process is continued until a consensus scenario is agreed upon.

School-Based Decision Making (SBDM): A model for school improvement that allows for building-level shared decision making; the vehicle through which research on what constitutes effective schools will be implemented (Kentucky Education Reform Act term).

School-Based Management (SBM): A structure and process that allows greater decision-making power related to the areas of instruction, budget, policies, rules and regulations, staffing, and all matters of governance; and a process that involves a variety of stakeholders in the decisions related to the local individual school building.

SBM Local School Councils: Representatively appointed or elected groups or teams of school stakeholders, frequently charged with substantial decision-making responsibility or substantial advisory capacities.

School Climate: A unique set of internal characteristics that affect the lives of those in a school; the tone or atmosphere.

School District Culture: The beliefs and values held, the standard processes and activities utilized, and the traditions maintained by both the students and the employees of the school district and by the community members who live within the geographical bounds of the school district.

School Improvement: Any systematic effort to improve the conditions of or the effects of schooling.

Shared Decision Making (SDM):   A collaborative decision-making process that involves multiple individuals representing different assignments within either the individual school or the different areas of the school district.

Simulations: Planning practice exercises designed to hone the skills of planners and prepare them for actual situations in strategic and tactical planning.

Soft Data: Data that are private and thus are not independently verifiable.

Stakeholders: The local community residents, including parents, students, or other persons who have an interest or stake in what takes place in the school district.

Strategic Goals: Goals that are derived from the vision and mission statement; they are the guidelines that indicate in detail what is to be achieved at some point in the future.

Strategic Planning: Long-term planning to achieve a future vision of "what could be" or "what should be"; proactive planning that identifies problems and opportunities for organizations.

Strategy: The design to achieve a clearly defined goal. It is the *what* to be achieved, while a tactic is the *how* or maneuvers used to achieve the goal.

SWOT Analysis: A process utilized by strategic planners to identify, collect, monitor, analyze, and synthesize data about the strengths, weaknesses, opportunities, and threats that exist both in the internal environment of the organization and in the external environment with which the organization interacts. These data are useful in planning strategies and tactics that both capitalize on strengths and opportunities and minimize or overcome weaknesses and threats in a manner that maximizes the possibility of achieving the organization's vision.

Systemic Change: The transformation of a social system through integration and mutual reinforcement.

Tactical Planning: Planning that details how to achieve the strategic goals developed by strategic planning.

Telstar: A consensus building technique that is similar to the Fishbowl Technique, but it allows for even broader participation. Telstar can be best used when very large, diverse stakeholders' groups have an interest in the planning results.

Total Quality Management (TQM): A customer-focused, strategy-driven approach that makes new and profound demands on every organization. TQM involves six basic principles: customer focus, focus on the process as well as the results, prevention versus inspection, mobilizing expertise of the work force, fact-based decision making, and feedback.

Transformational Change: A type of change that is dramatic in structure and radically changes organizational culture.

Trend Analysis: The process of using monitored data over a period of years to identify trends, then using these trends to predict future directions that should be considered when developing the strategic plan for the organization.

Vision: A clear mental picture or written statement of what the strategic planners expect or desire their organization to look like and deliver at some point in the future. It is the description of the planners' determination of "what should be" or "what can be" at some future date.

References

Allen, L., & Glickman, C. (1992). School improvement: The elusive faces of shared governance. *NASSP Bulletin, 76*(542), 80-87.

Ammon, S., & Plato, G. (1991). Total quality management: Is it just common sense? *Quality Digest, 11*(10), 81-88.

Banghart, F. W., & Trull, A., Jr. (1973). *Educational planning.* New York: Macmillan.

Bryson, J. (1988). *Strategic planning for public and nonprofit organizations: A guide to strengthening and sustaining organizational achievement.* San Francisco: Jossey-Bass.

Butterfield, R. (1991). Deming's 14 points applied to service. *Training, 28*(3), 50-59.

Carlson, R. V., & Awkerman, G. (1991). *Educational planning: Concepts, strategies, practices.* New York: Longman.

Cox, P. L., French, L. C., & Houcks-Horsley, S. (1987). *Getting the principal off the hotseat: Configuring leadership and support for school improvement.* Andover, MA: Regional Laboratory for Educational Improvement of the Northeast and Islands.

Crowson, R. L. (1992). *School-community relations, under reform.* Berkeley, CA: McCutchan.

Ferketish, B. (1991). A fly on the wall hears what executives say about TQM. *Quality Digest, 11*(11), 56-62.

Gilmore, J., & Lozier, G. (1987). Managing strategic planning: A systems theory approach. *Educational Planning, 6*, 12-23.

Hanson, E. M. (1991). *Educational administration and organizational behavior*. Boston: Allyn & Bacon.

Herman, J. J. (1989a). External and internal scanning: Identifying variables that affect your school. *NASSP Bulletin, 73*(520), 48-52.

Herman, J. J. (1989b). Map the trip to your district's future. *The School Administrator, 45*(9), 16, 18, 23.

Herman, J. J. (1989c). School business officials' roles in the strategic planning process (Part II). *School Business Affairs, 55*(3), 20, 22-24.

Herman, J. J. (1989d). Site-based management: Creating a vision and mission statement. *NASSP Bulletin, 73*(519), 79-83.

Herman, J. J. (1989e). Strategic planning: One of the changing leadership roles of the principal. *The Clearing House, 63*(2), 56-58.

Herman, J. J. (1990a). Action plans to make your vision a reality. *NASSP Bulletin, 74*(523), 14-17.

Herman, J. J. (1990b). School-based management. *Instructional Leader, III*(4) [Texas Elementary Principals and Supervisors Association], 1-4.

Herman, J. J. (1992). Total quality management basics: TQM comes to school. *School Business Affairs, 58*(4), 20-28.

Herman, J. J. (1993). *Holistic quality: Managing, restructuring, and empowering schools*. Newbury Park, CA: Corwin Press.

Herman, J. (in press). Total quality management basics: Potential applications for school districts. *School Business Affairs*.

Herman, J. J., & Herman, J. L. (1991). *The positive development of human resources and school district organizations*. Lancaster, PA: Technomic.

Herman, J. J., & Herman, J. L. (1993). *School-based management: Current thinking and practice*. Springfield, IL: Charles C Thomas.

Herman, J. J., & Kaufman, R. (1991). Making the mega plan. *American School Board Journal, 178*(5), 24, 25, 41.

Hoyle, J. R., English, F. W., & Steffy, B. E. (1990). *Skills for successful school leaders* (2nd ed.). Arlington, VA: American Association of School Administrators.

Hyde, A. (1990-1991). Rescuing quality measurement from TQM. *The Bureaucrat, 19*(4), 10, 17-19.

Jablonski, J. (1991). *Implementing total quality management: An overview.* San Diego: Pfeiffer.

Kaufman, R., & Herman, J. J. (1989). Planning that fits every district: Three choices help define your plan's scope. *The School Administrator, 46*(8), 17-19.

Kaufman, R., & Herman, J. J. (1991a). Strategic planning for a better society. *Educational Leadership, 48*(7), 4-8.

Kaufman, R., & Herman, J. J. (1991b). *Strategic planning in education: Rethinking, restructuring, and revitalizing.* Lancaster, PA: Technomic.

Keith, S., & Girling, R. H. (1991). *Education, management, and participation.* Boston, MA: Allyn & Bacon.

Levine, D. U. (1991). Creating effective schools: Findings and implications from research and practice. *Phi Delta Kappan, 72*(5), 389-393.

Lezotte, L. W. (Speaker). (1989). *Effective schools videotapes* (Videotapes). Okemos, MI: Effective Schools Products.

Mauriel, J. J. (1989). *Strategic leadership for schools: Creating and sustaining productive change.* San Francisco: Jossey-Bass.

McLagan, P. (1991). The dark side of quality. *Training, 28*(11), 31-33.

Melvin, C. (1991). Translating Deming's 14 points for education. *The School Administrator, 48*(9), 19, 20, 23.

Mercer, J. L. (1991). *Strategic planning for public managers.* New York: Quorum Books.

Milakovich, M. (1990). Total quality management for public sector productivity improvement. *Public Productivity and Management Review, 14*(1), 19-32.

Miller, L. R. (1974). *A peek at PERT.* Escondido, CA: The Center for Leadership Studies.

Paton, S. (1991). An interview with Curt W. Reimann. *Quality Digest, 11*(12), 43-48.

Poston, W. K. (1992). In times of scarcity, let the curriculum drive your budget. *The School Administrator, 6*(49), 18, 20-21.

Ryans, J., & Shanklin, W. (1985). *Strategic planning: Concepts and implementation.* New York: Random House.

Scherkenbach, W. (1991). *The Deming route to quality and productivity: Road maps and roadblocks.* Washington, DC: CEEP Press Books, George Washington University.

Schlechty, P. C. (1990). *Schools for the twenty-first century.* San Francisco: Jossey-Bass.

Scholes, G. W. (1991). KERA: A leadership (planning) challenge for school boards and superintendents. *Kentucky School Boards Association Journal, 10*(2), 15.

Steingraber, F. (1991). Total quality management: A new look at a basic issue. *Vital Speeches, 57*(13), 415-416.

Sui-Runyan, Y. & Hart, S. (1992). Management manifesto. *Executive Educator, 14*(1), 23-26.

Vincoli, J. (1991). Total quality management and the safety and health professional. *Professional Safety, 36*(6), 27-32.

Wilson, R., & Schmoker, M. (1992). Quest for quality. *Executive Educator, 14*(1), 18-22.

Zenger, W. F., & Zenger, S. K. (1992). *Curriculum planning: Outcomes-based accountability.* Saratoga, CA: R&E.

Index